Nicky Fifth

At the Jersey Shore

by Lisa Funari Willever

Franklin Mason Press
Trenton, New Jersey

For Todd, Jessica, Patrick, and Timothy, the reasons I write.
And for Molly Grace and Baby Maximus

A special thanks to Anne Salvatore, Wanda Swanson, and Iris
Hutchinson, three amazing NJ women.

Dedicated to Joey Angiolino and his amazing family.

Franklin Mason Press ISBN 978-0-9760469-8-1
Library of Congress Control Number: 2011925772

Editorial Staff: Faustiene Smith, Jennifer Wahner, Shoshana
Hurwitz, Linda Funari

FMP, Permissions Department,
PO Box 3808, Trenton, New Jersey, 08629
www.franklinmasonpress.com

Contents

The Nicky Fifth Series

written by
Award-winning Author Lisa Funari Willever
Winner of the 2009 Benjamin Franklin Award

Book One
32 Dandelion Court

Book Two
Garden State Adventure

Book Three
For Hire

Book Four
Passport to the Garden State

Book Five
At the Jersey Shore

A Letter from the Author

Dear Reader,

As the author of the Nicky Fifth books, I have learned as much about New Jersey as my readers. I consider myself a lucky author, as I must visit every place Nicky and T-Bone visit. To bring the Jersey Shore to life, my husband, Todd, my children, Jessica, Patrick, and Timothy, and I tried every beach, boardwalk, pizza, ice cream, and funnel cake. It's a tough job, but someone has to do it! The good news is that you can do it, also.

Let Nicky Fifth and T-Bone be your guide as you Explore the Shore. It's great to have a favorite beach, but don't let that stop you from visiting other beaches, too. My words can get you excited about the Jersey Shore, but words alone will never be a substitute for the real thing.

There has also been another very exciting development with the creation of the new www.nickyfifth.com website. We were very lucky to have the assistance of two College of New Jersey graduates, Allyssa Barnes and Andrew Sigwart. They have volunteered many hours to bring New Jersey to life. Andrew has edited Nicky and T-Bone's virtual video tours and Allyssa has created the interactive website.

You may have also noticed that this is the first time we have commissioned an actual portrait for the cover of the book and we would like to thank the award-winning artist, Lauren Lambiase, for capturing the true Nicky Fifth and T-Bone.

As with **Passport to the Garden State**, you will find a Passport in the back of this book, also. Read the story and talk your family into taking you on some great NJ day trips. *You'll thank them and they'll thank you.*

*As always, check the websites and call destinations ahead to be sure hours and offerings have not changed. While we are always sad to see a Stamp Stop close or go out of business, sadly, these things happen and are the risks of writing a book that blends fact and fiction. If a Stamp Stop is no longer operating, one of the other stops will stamp that box for you.

Enjoy New Jersey,
Lisa Funari Willever

Twenty-five cents from each book sold is donated to the Duke Pediatric Blood and Marrow Transplant Family Support Program to assist their work helping families in their time of need.

Chapter One
It's Official (*Almost)*

"Nicky," my mom hollered from the bottom of the stairs. "Nicky, you have a phone call."

"What?" I asked, even though I heard every word she said.

"I said that you have a phone call," she replied, suddenly appearing in the doorway with one eyebrow raised, one hand on her hip and the other hand holding a phone.

"Oh, sorry," I whispered. "Who is it?"

"It's Billy from the Governor's office," she mouthed as she handed me the phone.

"Hey, Billy, what's up?" I said, trying to sound like an adult.

"Good morning, Nicky. I hope I didn't wake you up," he started.

"No, my sisters took care of that," I explained.

"Great," he laughed. "Listen, the reason I'm calling you is because I received a phone call from the Governor regarding you and T-Bone."

Wow, I thought, suddenly wondering if T-Bone had been right and maybe the Governor did want to hire us to rake the leaves at Drumthwacket.

"Really?" I asked, curious since the Governor's official residence must have groundskeepers.

"Yes, as a matter of fact, you were the first item on the agenda this morning. We wanted to let you know that you may be getting a promotion."

"A promotion?" I asked.

"Well, your blog and website have become so popular with schools and families that the state of New Jersey would like to elevate you both to the more befitting status of *Official Junior Ambassadors*."

"Huh?" I asked, not sure what that even meant.

"Sorry," he laughed. "Several state Senators and members of the Assembly have approached the Governor about making you and T-Bone the *Official Junior Ambassadors of New Jersey.*"

"Really?" I asked, excited, but still confused. We hadn't been the *Unofficial Junior Ambassadors* all that long and I always thought it took years for people to get promotions.

"To be honest with you, Nicky, no one ever thought about New Jersey having any kind of junior ambassadors," he explained. "When I first heard you and T-Bone on the radio and mentioned it to the Governor, everyone just thought it would be a fun thing to do."

"It's been fun finding, visiting, and reporting about all of the great places in New Jersey," I agreed. "Especially since we had never even heard of most of the places we visited."

"That's why you're getting the promotions. Sadly, most of New Jersey's residents have never heard of these places and now, because of your reports, they're going out and exploring the state."

"Really?" I asked, shocked that something we were doing could make people do anything.

"Well, you boys have become very popular. We get phone calls from people asking where you'll visit next and even offering suggestions of places you should try."

"That's pretty cool. You know we get our best ideas from the people who live in the towns we visit," I added. "But I don't understand what you mean by *Official Junior Ambassadors*. Do we have to be elected?"

"No," Billy laughed. "You don't have to be elected. From what I understand, there are two bills to make you both official. One is in the Senate and the other is in the Assembly. It's really very exciting."

"Billy, I have to be honest with you. I have no idea what you're talking about. Do we owe the state money?"

"I'm sorry," he laughed. "You guys have done such a great job; sometimes I forget you're both kids!"

"That's all right," I said, hoping I wasn't going to have to give my dad a bill from the state of New Jersey, especially since they probably don't accept coupons or have instant rebates.

"We all feel that your work is very valuable. In fact, it's too valuable to have you serve as *Unofficial Junior Ambassadors* any longer. This bill will make you both Official. Do you get it now?"

"Kind of, but I don't know what you mean when you say the Senate and Assembly have bills," I admitted, quickly realizing every word he was saying must have had multiple meanings.

It took a few minutes, but Billy was able to explain exactly what was happening. Apparently, those two bills would be discussed by the Senate and the Assembly and then they would vote on them. If they passed by a simple majority, we would become *Official*. This is amazing, I thought. I wasn't sure who to tell first. As much as I wanted to run downstairs and tell my mom, I knew T-Bone had to be the first call. I dialed his number hoping he was home. Since he wasn't at my house, I knew it was almost a guarantee.

"At your service," answered T-Bone. "Thomas here."

"Hey, Thomas," I began, "I just got a call from Billy."

"Billy Venuto?" he asked.

"No, not Billy Venuto."

"Billy Anderson?" he tried again.

"No, why don't you just let me tell you," I insisted.

"Okay, I give up," he laughed. "Maybe you should just tell me."

"Billy from the Governor's office," I said.

"He called you? Why didn't he call me?" T-Bone wondered.

"Yeah, that's a real mystery," I answered sarcastically. "Anyway, he had some really big news."

"They're sending us to Hawaii?" he guessed.

"No," I said. "Why would they send New Jersey's *Official Junior Ambassadors* to Hawaii?"

"I wasn't talking about the official junior ambassadors, I was talking about us, the unofficial guys," he explained.

"Oh, that was his news," I started. "The Senate and the Assembly want to elevate us to *Official Junior Ambassadors*. Do you believe it?"

"Believe it? I don't even understand it," he laughed. "Is this good? Are they moving us upstairs?"

"Let me explain," I began, sounding like an expert, even though ten minutes earlier I didn't understand anything either. "It turns out that the state never really thought about junior ambassadors until Billy heard us on that NJ 101.5 radio show. When they asked us to be unofficial ambassadors they never expected what's happened."

"What's happened?" he asked.

"According to Billy, our reports have become pretty popular with kids and families and schools. People are visiting the places we write about and he said it's a lot of people."

"Seriously?" he asked, not sure if this was some sort of practical joke.

"Seriously," I confirmed.

"How do they know?" he wondered.

"I wondered about that, too," I said. "But Billy told me the state has received tons of phone calls and e-mails from people saying thank you for sending them to new places, asking where we're going next, and offering suggestions."

"Really?" he asked in amazement.

"Really," I answered. "But it gets better. The Senate and the Assembly want to, hold on, I wrote it down on a piece of paper, there it is, elevate us to the more befitting status of *Official Junior Ambassadors*."

"You mean they're going to pay us?" he exclaimed. "We're going pro! Does that mean they'll have an assembly at school for us?"

"No, no, no," I continued. "He didn't mention anything about money, but he said the two legislative bodies of our state government, the Senate and Assembly, will be voting on resolutions to change us from unofficial to official."

"What's a resolution?" he asked. "Is it a law?"

"No, I think it's like a declaration. The state will recognize us as the *Official Junior Ambassadors*."

"So, bottom-line this for me?" he said.

"What?" I asked.

"I don't know, my dad always says that when I'm about to ask for something but I start telling him a long story. I think it means get to the point."

"I just told you that we're going to change from unofficial to official," I said, understanding why his dad loses his patience.

"So, let's see," he said, "the state is not sending us to Hawaii, not paying us, and we're not going to be a law? Why is this better, again?"

"Because the state wants to use our pictures to let people know who we are and also to mark places we visit so families will know those places are great. Kind of like a seal of approval."

"So are we talking billboards? Murals on the sides of skyscrapers like they have in New York?" he wondered.

"I don't know exactly what the plan is," I admitted. "Billy said he would be in touch and that he had an idea for our next trips. He thought it would be great if we visited the Jersey Shore."

"We did that already," said T-Bone. "Remember when we went to Long Beach Island, Tuckerton, and Seaside?"

"Sure, but that was before we became any kind of ambassador. He wants us to visit all of the beaches, as New Jersey's pending *Official Junior Ambassadors*."

"How many beaches are we talking about, four or five?"

"127 miles of coastline," I laughed.

"127 miles?" he shrieked. "Are you kidding me?"

"That's right, 127 miles of sand meeting surf," I laughed. "But it gets better. They want to give us Flip Cams so we can videotape the places we visit and they'll put them on a website."

"No way, I always wanted a Flip Cam for when I learn to skateboard and snowboard," he said. "But won't this be like asking people to watch boring vacation videos?"

"No, think of it like a documentary. He said he wants the videos to bring New Jersey to life so kids, families, and schools can actually see different places in New Jersey."

"Kind of like the coming attractions at a movie?" he guessed. "Just seeing a few minutes makes you want to see more?"

"I guess we'll be like the coming attractions," I laughed.

"I have to be honest," he said. "I'm not a big fan of coming attractions. They say the movie will start at 7:00 and then they have 20 minutes' worth of previews before it starts. It only works out when you're running late or standing in a long snack line trying to buy a refillable popcorn, candy, soda, and ice cream."

"I don't think you have to worry; they're not showing our videos at the movies," I said.

"Good, then count me in," T-Bone declared. "Did they say where we should start?"

"No, but he gave me ideas people had sent in and they all sound fantastic. He said families can do day trips or get a hotel and string a few together. It's up to us, but it's also a big responsibility."

"That's good," he agreed. "I definitely think we're up to the challenge. When do the video cameras come?"

"This week," I replied. "So we don't have a lot of time to prepare. We should make a list and then start brainstorming. Maybe you should come over and we can start Googling the Jersey Shore."

Suddenly, the phone clicked. "Hello? Hello?" I asked. "T-Bone, are you there?"

There was no answer. That's weird, I thought. I guess we got disconnected. I decided to go downstairs and tell my mom about the news. Before I reached the bottom step, the doorbell was ringing. As my mom opened the door and T-Bone walked in, I realized we hadn't been disconnected at all.

I had been hung up on.

Chapter Two
I'll Just Take Them All

"Hey, Nick," said T-Bone, visibly out of breath. "What have you done so far?"

"What have I done?" I repeated. "You hung up on me two minutes ago. I made my bed and walked downstairs. That's what I've done."

"Clearly, you'll need to step it up a little if you want to be an *Official Junior Ambassador*," he scolded.

"What is he talking about?" asked my mom as she closed the front door. "Are you boys being promoted to official ambassadors?"

"Actually we're being elevated," said T-Bone. "I don't know if that means in a plane or an elevator, but Billy said somebody in Trenton wants to elevate us."

"Congratulations!" my mom exclaimed. "Boys, this is such an honor. Nicky, why didn't you tell me?"

"Because I'd have to have wings to beat T-Bone. I was coming down to tell you when the doorbell rang."

"Well, I want to hear all about it," she smiled.

As we started to explain everything, my mom's eyes started to get teary.

"Mrs. A., are you crying?" T-Bone asked, making another obvious observation.

"I'm just so proud of you both," she sniffled. "I never thought anyone was taking your work so seriously. I can't believe there's a resolution with your names on it."

"Two of them," corrected T-Bone. "But, they're still not paying us."

"Boys, you are getting something far more valuable than money," said my mom.

"A car?" gasped T-Bone. "Are they giving us each a car? How did you know? When did they call you? Did they call my mom yet?"

My mom stopped crying and just stared at T-Bone for a minute. "Tommy, why would they give cars to a couple of young kids who don't even drive?"

"I don't know," he shrugged. "Why would they give us two bills and say we don't owe them money? Politics is all very mysterious."

My mom and I both rolled our eyes. "No, Tommy," she said. "They're giving you opportunities. You have the opportunity to really see your state, all of it, and that's something most people take for granted. But you're also motivating families to spend time together exploring New Jersey. You have something very valuable: a chance to make a difference."

"Oh, and they're giving us Flip Cams," he smiled. "So basically we're getting opportunities and video cameras. Not bad, huh?"

While my mom excused herself to restore her sanity, T-Bone and I hit the computer. I hadn't realized it before, but New Jersey has an enormous number of beach towns. From Cape May to Sandy Hook, it was one town after another. And as we surfed their websites we realized that even though they were all coastal towns, each town had its own personality. Some were big and loud, with boardwalks, rides, and thousands of sunbathers under giant umbrellas, and some were smaller and quieter with hardly any tourists. Then there were those that seemed as though no one really knew they existed, almost like hidden treasures. I wondered if the few people who know about those towns would appreciate us sharing their towns with the rest of the state.

As we continued our research, furiously writing ideas in our New Jersey notebooks, I realized my mom was right. We did have an amazing opportunity. We were like Ponce de Leon and Henry Hudson, sort of. The only difference was they explored places that were *undiscovered* and we were exploring places that were *unremembered*. It seemed silly that New Jersey, the most densely populated of all the states, could have so many forgotten places. My dad always said it was because people were just too busy nowadays and didn't have time to look for new places. Of course, my mom always corrected him and said that people had time, they just didn't make time. Apparently, my mom was right. If everything Billy said was true, then people just needed to be reminded and then they would make time.

Two hours into our research my mom asked us to take a ride. While we initially resisted, it was clear that she wasn't really asking, but was telling us to get in the car.

"Where are we going?" I asked, knowing that she knew we didn't have a minute to waste. "We're not going shopping, are we?"

"No," she smiled. "I had a couple of ideas that I thought might help you."

"It's not going to take long, is it?"

"Not at all," she said as she turned onto the New Jersey Turnpike.

"Mom, you know you're on the turnpike, right?" I asked, completely aware that my dad would do anything to avoid paying tolls.

My mom pretended not to hear me. As we headed down the turnpike, I saw a sign for a rest stop.

"Hey, Mrs. A.," said T-Bone, "do you think we could stop?"

"You need a rest after ten minutes?" I asked. "What are you, four years old?"

"No, but I drank a bottle of water as I was running over to your house."

"Of course you did," I mumbled, wondering what else he was able to squeeze into a two-minute run.

"Actually, that's where we're going," my mom smiled as she glided off into the exit lane, weaving around a shoulder full of trucks and a van that had trouble deciding if it was a car or a truck.

"Are you kidding me?" I asked, even more confused.

"You paid to drive to a rest stop. Dad's gonna be furious."

"Follow me," my mom laughed. "This will only take a few minutes."

While T-Bone ran in the restroom, I wondered if my mom was feeling all right. It was almost impossible to get my dad to pull into a rest stop because he always said letting six people out of the van eats up too much driving time. He was wrong. Getting six people back into a van is what affected his driving time and, for my dad, making good time was an essential part of any trip. I wondered if she got some kind of coupon for one of the restaurants and didn't feel like cooking. That better be some coupon, I thought. When I turned around to ask her why we were here, she was standing at the Travel and Tourism desk, speaking to the woman who worked there.

"I believe everything you need is right on these two walls," the woman smiled. "We're happy to have the boys' help."

"Thanks," said my mom as she pulled out a tote bag from her purse.

"Mom, what are we doing?" I asked, as T-Bone re-joined us.

"We're gathering brochures for as many beach towns as we can," she explained. "This way, you'll have something in hand and get a better idea of what each town is about."

"This is an awesome idea," T-Bone nodded. "How did you think of it?"

"Do you remember when we moved to New Jersey and Nicky had his heart set on a Florida vacation?" she asked. "Sure, I remember," T-Bone nodded.

"Well, when we realized we could never afford to bring the family to Florida, we came here to see what New Jersey had to offer. We filled up a bag of brochures and then…"

"And then you used them to cut out pictures and turn that science fair board into a Garden State Adventures board," I said, finishing her sentence.

"That's right," T-Bone added, "I forgot about that board and remember Nick wasn't happy about seeing Jersey."

"I know," said my mom. "Do you remember how upset he was? And now look, he's like Mr. New Jersey."

"Without the muscles," T-Bone laughed.

"In my defense," I began, "I didn't know anything about this state. Everyone told me horror stories. My friends in Philly told me I would spend the summer pumping gas and collecting tolls. And I was moving from the very cool-sounding Fifth Street to Dandelion Court."

"Isn't that the biggest irony?" my mom sighed. "People have no idea how beautiful, interesting, and amazing New Jersey is and sadly, that includes most of the people who live here."

"Not for long," T-Bone said as he methodically grabbed every shore brochure, one row at a time. "Hey, look, they even have a catalog of places for the whole state."

"You should also check out the *Kid Stuff* coupon book that we order from the school fundraiser. I bet they have coupons for many of the activities, restaurants, and stores you are sending people to visit," my mom suggested. "And don't forget the *Entertainment Book*. Those coupons can really help families save money while enjoying the state."

"Good point," I agreed.

When we finished collecting the brochures we thanked the woman and headed back home. We wanted to have some more trips planned before the video cameras arrived and decided to start at the bottom and work our way up. Exit 1 on the Garden State Parkway is Cape May, the southernmost point in the state, and it seemed like number one was always a good place to start.

As much as I wanted to read the brochures in the car, reading in a moving car sometimes made me feel sick. I decided to wait until we got in the house. We pulled out the Cape May brochures and pulled up Cape May web-sites. It looked amazing. They had a ferry to Delaware that even cars could ride on, a free zoo, beaches, Victorian houses, a historic village and whale watching. We had to really do our homework so we could plan a day that didn't have us driving back and forth all day and didn't try to squeeze too much in. The easier we made it for us, the easier it would be for everyone that followed our itinerary. It was my civic duty to get this right.

We spent about three hours reading brochures, following up on websites, and making a schedule. By the time we were finished, my dad was walking in from what looked like another hard day at work.

"Hey, guys," he said, missing his usual pep.

"Hey, Mr. A., we've got some good news for you," T-Bone said, sure my dad would be excited.

"That's great," my dad answered and kept walking.

"What's wrong with your pop?" asked T-Bone, disappointed that my dad didn't hear a word he said.

"I don't know," I said, hoping he wouldn't ask any more questions. My dad, the produce manager at the supermarket, the man who loves fruits and vegetables so much, was waiting to hear if his company was going to have to sell their stores. The economy was bad and business had been so slow, he was really worried about the future. I decided this was definitely not the time to tell him our news and definitely not the time to mention our trip on the turnpike.

Before T-Bone left I called my grandfather to tell him the news and ask if he could take us to Cape May. Unlike my dad, his reaction was not a disappointment. He was very proud and very excited and agreed to take us to Exit 1 as soon as the video cameras arrived. I called Billy to tell him and he said he knew we would hit the ground running and he would let the Governor know. Wow, I thought, I can't believe the Governor will know where we are. Of course, since we had never met, the Governor didn't really even know who we are, but it was all set.

Billy said the cameras would arrive in two days and that they were so simple a first grader could use them. That concerned me a little since every time a salesman told my father something was so easy a first grader could use, it never worked out so well. I always thought they should actually send that first grader along to set things up. Hopefully, this would be easier than the digital camera, the wireless printer, the router, and my mom's pedometer that still beeps every day at noon.

When the delivery truck arrived, T-Bone came over and spent two hours installing the software and charging the batteries. It turned out that T-Bone was that first grader. He had a knack for the technical and before I knew it, we were up and running. The camera couldn't have been easier: press the red button to record, press the red button to stop, and press the garbage can to delete. And when we plugged the camera into the computer, all of our practice videos were right there, ready to be edited into movies or uploaded for Billy. The most impressive thing was the two letters on official state letterhead from the Governor, thanking New Jersey's soon-to-be *Official*

Junior Ambassadors for their service.

"I'll take that," my mom said, carefully grabbing the letters out of our hands.

"Scrapbook?" I asked.

"No, sweetie," she shook her head. "Scrapbooks are for movie stubs and report cards. Letters from Governors go into frames."

As T-Bone left to go home my mother came running out of the kitchen waving two frames in her hands.

"Here, Tommy, don't forget this," she said, handing him a framed copy of his letter from the Governor.

"Thanks, Mrs. A.," he smiled proudly.

"You're welcome," she winked, taking my dad's favorite golf picture off the wall and replacing it with my letter. "He'll never notice."

I spoke to my grandfather and it was all set. He would pick us up at 6 a.m. and we'd be on our way to Cape May.

Chapter Three
Cape May

Like most senior citizens, my grandfather woke up early and was always on time. If you told him a party started at 4:00, he was at your door at 4:00, on the button, as he liked to say. Today was no different. At five of six I went downstairs and my mom was sitting on the bottom step.

"Hey, why are you sitting on the steps?" I asked.

"I was on the internet trying to see if they had any news about your father's store," she sighed.

"Did they?" I asked.

"No, honey, not yet," she managed a worried smile. "But I'm sure it'll all work out. It always does."

Before I could answer, I could see the lights from my

grandfather's car. I felt bad leaving my mom since she looked worried, but she jumped up, gave me a kiss and told me to have a great day and take lots of video.

I jumped in my grandfather's car and we drove the 30 seconds to T-Bone's house. He was waiting with his mother by the front door and we did a double-take when he came out. He was carrying a duffle bag, two boogie boards, a beach chair and an umbrella.

"You moving to Cape May?" my grandfather laughed.

"Well, you can never be too prepared," he nodded. "I don't know what we'll end up doing, but this should cover everything. My mom said if we have time to go in the water we should have a chair and umbrella for your grandfather and towels and sunscreen…"

"I get it," I laughed. "Now, get in the car!"

We drove south down Route 206 and passed some really nice diners. My grandfather told us New Jersey had over 600 diners and was the diner capital of the world. I was starting to believe it. When we hit Route 30 in Hammonton, the blueberry capital of the world, my grandfather said we could go left to Atlantic City or hop on the Atlantic City Expressway to get to the Garden State Parkway. Since we were in a hurry to get there, we picked the Expressway. It sounded quicker.

While we drove, we discussed the itinerary. We planned to concentrate on history first. Cape May has an amazing history and we decided to drive down Washington Street to see the historic Victorian houses. We could take a tour and were really excited to check out the Emlen Physick Estate. Our next stop would be Historic Cold Spring Village, a re-enactment of a rural community in the mid-19th century. This open-air, living history museum was right up our alley, as you didn't just see the buildings, but you were able to speak with the re-enactors and see what life was like back then. I just hoped they were prepared for T-Bone. Next, we wanted to stop by the Cape May Zoo. Since it was free, we figured it wouldn't take long and then we would check out the lighthouse, the Cape May-Lewes Ferry, and then maybe the beach. My grandfather said it was an ambitious plan, but luckily he was always up for a challenge.

As we drove into Cape May, I could hear the seagulls and smell the salt air. It was a sunny day but not unbearably hot or humid, and we found Washington Street right away. The houses were like mansions and I really did feel like we were dropped into a time machine. I could imagine women with their dresses, hats and umbrellas walking around and men swimming in their bathing suits that started at their shoulders and ended at their ankles. The town was so historic that it was one of the few towns to be designated a National Historic Landmark.

With a map in hand, T-Bone led us to the Emlen Physick Estate, a four-acre historic site in the center of Cape May located at 1048 Washington Street. Built in 1879, it was Cape May's only historic house museum. Like Lucy the Elephant, it was also saved from being demolished.

"So what's with this Physick House?" asked T-Bone.

"Well, the brochure says that a visit to the Physick Estate today offers a look back at our Victorian past as evidenced by its architecture, decorative arts, customs, and the lives of one particular Cape May family, the Physicks. Emlen Physick Jr., his widowed mother, Frances Ralston, and his maiden aunt Emilie Parmentier moved into their home when it was completed in 1879."

"I guess you would have to be a doctor to afford an estate," T-Bone commented. "What kind of doctor was he? Plastic surgeon?"

"I don't think they did a lot of plastic surgery back then," my grandfather laughed. "Back then they concentrated more on things like survival."

"It says here that he never practiced medicine," I read aloud.

"Oh, a natural," said T-Bone, "some guys just go straight to the major leagues."

"No, not practice like he's learning," my grandfather corrected. "Practicing medicine is what all doctors who see patients do. I assume he studied medicine but had a different career."

"You're right, Pop," I agreed. "His grandfather, Dr. Philip Syng Physick, was a famous doctor from Philadelphia and he was considered the father of modern surgery. Emlen graduated from medical school, but led the life of a Gentleman Farmer."

"Wow, he must have liked fruits and vegetables as much as your dad to give up medicine for farming."

"Coming from a wealthy family, I'm sure he wasn't outside with a hoe," my grandfather laughed.

"It says here that he owned two tenant farms and kept livestock at the estate," I continued to read.

As we entered the house, it was clear that the Physick family was definitely wealthy. The tour was amazing and we could really see what it would have been like to live in the Victorian era. A woman told us that they also had trolley tours that go through the town. While we didn't have enough time to try it, I wrote the words *trolley tour* in my notebook and put a big star in front of it.

While T-Bone operated the Flip Cam, I took notes. As we left, we saw brochures for ghost tours, murder mysteries, craft shows and special events. I even noticed that they had a place called the Twinings Tea Room and knew that a tea room would definitely get my mom's attention. When we returned to the car, I tried to picture Cape May in the early 1900s. It was times like this that I really wished I had a time machine.

Our next stop was Historic Cold Spring Village. From the brochure we grabbed at the rest stop, it looked like our kind of place and we couldn't wait to get there.

"Here we are," said my grandfather as he pulled into the parking lot.

There were 22 acres of shaded lanes, just like the brochure said, and in addition to a collection of late 18th- and 19th-century buildings saved from demolition by their relocation; I could see costumed re-enactors throughout the village. This time I shot the video and left T-Bone to do the talking. While we looked at our map, a woman asked if we needed help finding anything. Her name was Patricia Salvatore but she said we could call her Anne. It turned out that our new friend, Anne, was the director.

"Wow, that's kind of like the mayor," T-Bone whispered.

Not only was she the director, Anne and her husband, Joe, co-founded the village. By the time T-Bone was done quizzing her, we learned that they had been instrumental in saving many pieces of New Jersey history. Growing up in Cape May, Joe even worked to create the Naval Air Station Wildwood Aviation Museum out of an old wooden hangar that had been scheduled for demolition.

After T-Bone explained our pending promotions to *Official Junior Ambassadors*, he asked her how she found the time to do so many great things.

"You make time when something is important," she smiled. "And history teaches us about the future."

"You mean the past," said T-Bone.

"No, dear," she continued, "the past is the best guide to the future. That is exactly why we must work to preserve our state's amazing history."

"It seems like you've saved a lot of it," T-Bone said as he looked around. "Do you think there's anything left for kids to save?"

"I wish I could say that every valuable historic landmark was safe, but unfortunately, so many of them are in danger of closing. We could use the help of every person in New Jersey, especially kids."

"I love history," T-Bone explained. "And I love the present saving the future through the past. But I still don't know what I should do."

"Well, when you become *Official Junior Ambassadors* you can share these wonderful places with the state and encourage families to take advantage of them," she suggested. "That support will ensure their survival. You will be a great ally to history."

By saying those words to T-Bone, it was almost as if she had knighted him. Suddenly, he had a title, *T-Bone of New Jersey, Ally to History*. We thanked Anne for her time and set off to visit the buildings and soak in the early American atmosphere. We talked to a blacksmith, a bookbinder, and a broommaker, made a craft, saw some farm animals and even grabbed some ice cream. The people we spoke with didn't just teach us things we didn't know, they taught us *interesting things* we didn't know. I thought it was amazing that each one of these buildings was saved from another south Jersey location and moved to the village. Before we left we checked out the country store and realized it was almost noon.

"Are you boys hungry?" asked my grandfather.

"I am," I whispered as I continued to film. "Where do you want to eat?"

"I don't know about you, but I'm in the mood for something historic," added T-Bone.

"You want to eat something old?" I asked sarcastically.

"Yeah, definitely. No, wait, not old like stale food. Like food early Americans would have eaten, but not like a rabbit or a squirrel…"

"How about the Old Grange Restaurant?" my grandfather said, pointing to a large white building. "This building was the first that Anne and Joe acquired and it's from 1867. Is that historic enough for you, Tommy?"

"As long as the food is from the present, I'm in," said T-Bone.

Everyone enjoyed the lunch as much as the setting and we left the village knowing we would definitely be back to spend the day during one of their theme weekends. Our next stop was the Cape May Zoo. While I wasn't much of a zoo guy, probably from the million times we visited the Philadelphia Zoo, we had a duty to check everything out. Since it was free, I was expecting something along the lines of a small petting zoo: goats, donkeys, chickens, and a few horses. I had no idea that this was a real zoo.

As I opened the map I realized just how wrong I was and started filming. The zoo had everything from camels and birds to lions and zebras to alligators and bears. We walked on elevated, boardwalk-style bridges and I found myself enjoying it.

"Hey, Nick, I can't believe your father hasn't found this place yet. You don't even need a coupon." T-Bone laughed, referring to my father's frugalness.

I laughed, but at the same time remembered how down my father had been. I hated to see him so worried about his job. Maybe hearing about a free zoo would cheer him up. And there was a gift shop, so I knew my mom would definitely like it. I made another note in my notebook.

When we left the zoo it was getting pretty hot and humid; it was a typical New Jersey summer day. It was time to head to the beach. Luckily, T-Bone brought a chair and umbrella for my grandfather and we were content messing around on the boogie boards. Since I met T-Bone, I had learned a lot about him: he has unusually good luck, a knack for stating the obvious, and the gift of gab. Today, I learned that he was absolutely useless on a boogie board. Never before had I seen a person fall so many times and keep going back for more.

"I'll give him this," my grandfather laughed as I sat down next to him, "he sure is determined."

I suddenly wondered if T-Bone's unusually good luck was really just perseverance. A massive wave knocked him over and I decided the jury was still out on that one.

As it got later, the crowds started thinning out. Just when I thought my grandfather was about to suggest leaving, he surprised me.

"You know, Nicky, this is my favorite time of day for the beach. It's quieter, the sun hangs a little lower, and you realize how lucky we are to live so close to an ocean."

"I never thought about it like that," I admitted. "You know, if you just look at the ocean, it's one of the few things that looks exactly like it did 100 years ago. We're seeing the same exact thing Victorian era kids saw."

"Pretty amazing, huh?" my grandfather said as he sunk back into T-Bone's chair. "Next time, we can try whale watching, too."

We decided to visit the Cape May Lighthouse and the World War II Lookout Tower on Sunset Boulevard, New Jersey's last freestanding World War II tower. We climbed to the tower's sixth floor spotting gallery and learned about homeland defense efforts during the war. After a while we headed to the Washington Street Mall. Unlike the average mall, it was all outdoors and the shops and restaurants were very unique. The streets were decorated with lampposts and a gazebo was nearby where old fashioned music could often be heard. We went to a fun restaurant called the Ugly Mug and discussed our day. I couldn't wait to get home and look over the videos we shot. Since T-Bone did a lot of filming, I was hoping the videos would come out alright.

Luckily, Flip Cams don't have a lens cap.

Chapter Four
Wildwood

We were still exhausted from our fun in Cape May, but we were on a mission and ready to plan our next trip. Going in order, our next destination was the Wildwoods which included North Wildwood, Wildwood, and Wildwood Crest.

Cape May was historic, but Wildwood had a completely different atmosphere. With five miles of wide, free beaches and an amazing two-and-a-half mile boardwalk, it looked like it would definitely live up to its name. We downloaded our Cape May videos and started our Wildwood research. My mom's brochures, along with the internet, made the research fun, something I never thought I'd say.

Since T-Bone was such a stickler for history, I looked up Wildwood's long history. I read that the first recorded description was over 350 years ago and it was called the

Island of Five Mile Beach. That's not very original, I thought. By 1870, a few fishermen became the first white settlers and built shacks on the north end of the island and in 1874 the government built a lighthouse at Hereford Shoals.

The story of modern Wildwood began in 1880 when a man concerned about his wife's health was advised to take her to the beach. This gentleman joined several other families and, in 1885, Holly Beach Borough was incorporated. Soon the newly formed boroughs of Wild-wood and Holly Beach merged into the City of Wildwood. The old black and white pictures in the brochures and on the websites were amazing. The color pictures of the modern Wildwoods were as amazing.

T-Bone came by as usual, around lunchtime, but didn't seem like himself.

"What's the matter?" I asked.

"I did some research and I don't think Wildwood has any history," he said. "Sure they have water parks, a boardwalk and beaches, but I'm worried there may not be any history. Now that I'm a *Great Ally to History*, I have to think about these things."

"You don't think they just invented Wildwood, do you?" I laughed, remembering a time when he thought history was really, really boring.

"What do you mean?" he asked. "Did you find some history?"

"Every town in New Jersey has great history. We were one of the original thirteen colonies," I reminded him. "And yes, I found some interesting history."

"Do they have a lighthouse?" he wondered.

"Here," I said, handing him a brochure, "take a look."

We finished our research and my mom volunteered to take us on this particular day trip. My sisters were going to my grandparents' house and my brother, Timmy, would join us. Timmy wasn't so much a history buff as he was a water park and beach buff, and I think T-Bone was determined to change that.

Very early on Thursday morning, we pulled up in front of T-Bone's house and he appeared with his umbrella, beach chair, and boogie boards. The Flip Cam was charged and we were on our way. We followed the same exact route, 206 South to the Atlantic City Expressway to the Garden State Parkway. We got off at Exit 6 and followed Route 147 to North Wildwood. Our first stop was the Hereford Lighthouse and, because of its history, I knew T-Bone would love it. Unlike the traditional tower lighthouses, this one was housed in a cottage and looked like one of the Victorian homes in Cape May. We took a tour and learned about the life of a lighthouse keeper in the late 19th and early 20th centuries. While it was a very

41

important job, I didn't think I'd ever want to live at my work. Of course, on the way out, my mom stopped by the gift shop and picked up some postcards and a book to show my dad and sisters. I was pretty sure she had a t-shirt for herself, but when I looked in the bag, it was just postcards and a book. I figured she already hid it in her purse. Timmy liked it so much, he talked T-Bone into going to the top a second time while I went to get some video of the outside and gardens.

My mom suggested hitting the beach in Wildwood, but I remembered my grandfather's theory and talked her into trying a water park first, beach later. Morey's Pier had two water parks, Ocean Oasis and Raging Waters. We were discussing which water park to visit when a woman on a nearby bench joined our conversation.

"Excuse me, I couldn't help but hear your conversation," she said with a smile. "I may be able to help you."

"We love help," said T-Bone. "What've you got for us?"

"Well, if you plan to go on the rides later, you can buy a Morey's Pier combination pass. You can visit both water parks and ride all of the rides for one price. Since there are four of you, you can save more money with the Family Four Pack."

"Really," my mom nodded. "That definitely seems like the way to go."

"It's probably too much money," I whispered.

"It's okay, Nicky," my mom winked. "Your grandfather's really proud of how you boys are taking this job so seriously. He left money for all three of you to visit the water parks and the rides."

"Really?" I asked, wondering how my non-official younger brother scored money, too.

"Really," she smiled. "You can't write about the water parks if you don't try them, can you?"

And with that we headed to Raging Waters. There were so many things to do that we didn't know where to start. Luckily my mom loved water slides so we hit the Shotgun Falls, Rocket Rafts, and Speed Slides. After that, we took a leisurely ride on the Endless River.

"This is the life," T-Bone joked as he floated by me.

"You said it," I agreed, completely exhausted and happy to float along the river.

"Who's ready for more slides?" asked Timmy.

"How about we take some video and then head over to the other water park," my mom suggested, cleverly extending our break.

We didn't want to leave, but we were excited to see what

the other water park had to offer. Even though we were exhausted, we could never be too tired for a water park, so we headed to the Ocean Oasis.

"Mom, I hate to sound like T-Bone," Timmy started, "but are we going to eat today?"

"Oh, my goodness," my mom shrieked. "We're having so much fun that I forgot about lunch."

"Wow, I must be having fun," said T-Bone, "because I forgot, too."

"Hey, how about there?" I said, pointing to a place called Captain Jack's Café.

"Sounds good," T-Bone nodded, "but I'm treating."

"What?" I asked, knowing T-Bone was as broke as I was.

"My mom gave me money and said if your mom doesn't let me pay for the activities that I should pay for lunch."

"No, no, Tommy," my mom protested. "That's sweet, but not necessary."

"I'm sorry, Mrs. A.," T-Bone explained, "but my mom won't let me come if I'm sponging off of you guys."

Good thing my dad wasn't with us. That offer may have been too much for him to resist.

"Let the man pay," said Timmy, rubbing his stomach.

We all stopped and looked at my brother, but he had a point. My mom would have said the same thing if it was me, so she finally agreed. Of course, she tried to order the least expensive thing while Timmy went another direction, and ordered several things.

"Boy, that kid can eat," T-Bone shook his head as he forked over his mother's money.

"Funny," I said, "this is the most I've ever seen him eat."

When we finally finished eating we headed over to the Ocean Oasis. It was just as amazing as the first park. We hit the slides over and over and then found our way to their endless river. I had no idea who invented this shallow, winding path called the endless river, but this person was a genius. We must have lapped the park at least four times when I realized my mom and T-Bone were asleep in their tubes. Timmy, on the other hand, was spinning in his tube so fast that he was blurry.

Eventually, my mom woke up and suggested getting our gear from the car and hitting the beach.

"Your mom's a machine," said T-Bone. "Most parents would be waving the white flag by now."

"She's just getting started," I laughed.

We collected our beach gear and started our trek across the widest beach I had ever seen. I remembered reading that Wildwood had one of the widest beaches in the world, over 1,000 feet wide at some parts.

"No erosion here," T-Bone noticed.

"Definitely not," I agreed.

"Wow, my feet feel like they're on fire," said T-Bone as he started skipping and hopping.

"Why don't you put your shoes on?" I asked what seemed like a normal question.

"And get sand in them?" he gasped.

"What's the big deal?" I asked, still wearing my shoes.

"My mom goes nuts if we track dirt, mud, or sand in the house. If I showed up with sandy shoes, she'd probably send me to your house," he insisted.

"Better keep hopping," my mom laughed, saying exactly what my dad would have said. Except I was pretty sure she was joking. T-Bone didn't get it, but Timmy and I started cracking up.

"Oh, wow," he exclaimed. "I don't think my feet have ever been this hot. I can't wait to stick them in the ocean."

"What ocean?" Timmy asked in a spooky voice.

"That ocean right there," T-Bone pointed.

"I think you're so hot, you're seeing mirages," Timmy said in his most serious voice. "There's no ocean, that's a shopping center."

T-Bone stopped in his tracks and surveyed the entire scene. We all stopped as he determined whether or not the ocean in front of him was real. After a few seconds, his hot feet decided the only way to know was to go. He dropped everything and ran the last hundred feet. We grabbed his stuff and went a little closer to the water to set up. As Timmy and I opened the umbrella and dug a hole in the sand, T-Bone was jumping up and down in the water.

"It's real," he hollered. "Tell Timmy it's real."

"It's real," I sarcastically told my brother.

"Thanks," he sarcastically answered.

"You know, this is a nice time of day to sit on the beach," my mom observed as she sunk into T-Bone's chair.

"You don't say," I smirked. My grandfather was right, it was quiet and relaxing. I took one of the boogie boards and decided to lay on it, under the umbrella. I was so exhausted from the water parks I couldn't imagine getting up. T-Bone and Timmy, however, must have caught a second wind. I looked up and they were standing on the other boogie boards. That lasted three seconds. With each wave they were tossed around the beach, never standing up more than five seconds in a row. Just watching them was painful so I decided it was my turn for a nap. When I woke up, Timmy and T-Bone were high-fiving each other and yelling. I wondered if I had missed something cool.

"What happened?" I asked.

"You missed it," Timmy yelled. "We did six."

"Six what?" I asked, wondering if it was some awesome surfing move.

"Six seconds," they yelled.

I went back to sleep.

By 6:30, my mom put her book away and asked who was hungry.

"That depends," said T-Bone. "Who's paying?"

"Don't worry," my mom smiled. "I've got dinner. Let's eat on the boardwalk and then you boys can start going on some rides."

"Really?" I asked. "I thought it would be too late."

"Well, if you're too tired, we can go home," she shrugged.

"No way," Timmy yelled.

We dried off, grabbed some Jersey Shore pizza and checked out the almost two-mile boardwalk. Luckily, my mom didn't want us to walk it from end to end. After our first few steps we came face-to-face with a New Jersey icon: the tram car. All along the boardwalk you can hear the expression Wildwood made famous, "*Watch the tram car, please.*" Despite the constant warnings, T-Bone was almost run over seven times. Ironically, three of the near-misses were almost head-on crashes.

"Hey, T-Bone, try looking up," Timmy reprimanded. "It's starting to get embarrassing every time they almost run you over."

"He'll be okay; he's just tired. I know what he needs," my mom said, oblivious to just how tired he was. "Nothing gets your blood pumping like a roller coaster."

I couldn't believe it; she really was a machine. While we were all starting to fade, she was prodding us to keep going. T-Bone suggested we start heading home because it would be a long drive for her. My mom laughed and got into another line. I had taken so much video, I only had about ten minutes left. Suddenly I remembered we still needed to see the Crest.

"That's okay," said my mom. "We'll check it out."

It was amazing how different Wildwood was from Cape May, and how we loved them both. As we drove through the Crest, I noticed the hotels seemed like they were all part of some theme. My mom explained that they were all the hotels from the 1950s, or as they called it, the Doo Wop times. It looked like many of them were being restored. It also looked like my mom had a particular destination in mind. Soon, we stopped in front of a large brown house.

"Are we out of gas?" asked Tommy.

"No," my mom laughed.

"You're too tired to drive, aren't you?" T-Bone guessed. "I knew it would hit you. I just didn't think it would hit you while we were still in Wildwood."

"Not at all," said my mom. "See this house? This is where my family stayed when I was a kid."

"Really?" asked T-Bone. "Wildwood was around then?"

"Watch it," my mom laughed.

"What was it like back in the, I mean, then?" T-Bone caught himself before he said *old days.*

"Just like it is now; a great place. And the beaches are

free, so families don't have to spend much money to have a great day. We used to make sandwiches, pack a cooler, and spend the day on the free beaches. There were days that we probably didn't spend a dime."

"They say women marry men who remind them of their father," said T-Bone, not-so-subtly suggesting my grandfather and father were equally cheap.

"What was your favorite part, Mom?" asked Timmy.

"The whole experience," she answered.

"So, the beach or the boardwalk?" I asked.

"The whole thing," she explained, "the warm salt air, the sounds of the waves crashing, the seagulls, the lights on the boardwalk, and the smells of the pizza and cotton candy."

"So basically, the shore?" T-Bone laughed.

"No, Tommy," said my mom, "*the Jersey Shore.*"

Chapter Five
Stone Harbor, Avalon, and Sea Isle City

While our soon-to-be official job was fantastic, T-Bone and I realized we weren't paying too much attention to *At Your Service,* our odd-job business, and we were both broke. Some of our neighbors had left messages, so we decided to spend the day setting up appointments. We had a good number of customers and luckily they were patient. Mr. Delmo needed us to help him clean his garage and the Morrisons needed help changing batteries in their smoke detectors. We weren't making a million dollars, but we liked earning our own money. The jobs were always different and our customers appreciated our hard work ethic, as they called it. Some even said we would have survived the Great Depression. I wasn't sure what they meant, but I was pretty sure it was a compliment. By the end of the week, we were exhausted but a little richer, and we started to plan our next day trip. I pulled out my New Jersey map and determined the next stops would be Stone Harbor and Avalon. I had never heard of them and wondered if they had historic Victorian houses or a boardwalk full of games and rides. I soon realized they had neither, but that they were extremely popular with many people. It turned out their charm had nothing to do with history and activity. Instead, they were quiet and relaxing. I figured people should see every beach, but we'd need more activity on this trip. I decided to add Sea Isle City, the next beach town. I used my mom's brochures and the internet to get a good idea of what we should do during our visit. As I was putting my supplies away, the doorbell rang.

"Come on in, Tommy," my mom said as she swung the front door open.

"Here's your mail," he said, handing her a stack of envelopes. "It looks like it's mostly bills."

"Thanks," she said, nodding her head.

"You know you can lower your interest rates on your credit card today," he continued. "Thanks to your excellent credit, you've been pre-approved."

"Really?" my mom asked, curious as to what else T-Bone had read. "Is that all?"

"Oh, no," he remembered, "thanks for reminding me. You also need to renew your cookbook membership and if you act now you'll get a towel set as a free gift."

"You know it's really not polite to read other people's mail," my mom said in a gentle tone, knowing T-Bone didn't mean any harm.

"You're right. It's a federal offense, but I think that only counts for strangers," he assured her. "I'm pretty much family."

"Pretty much," she smiled, too tired to continue the conversation.

"Hey, don't forget you have a dentist appointment next week," he yelled, as she disappeared into the kitchen.

"What are you talking about?" I asked.

"Your mom and I were just going over the mail. How's the research coming along?"

"Good," I said. "I think I have our next trip planned."

"So where are we going?"

"Well, the next beach towns are Stone Harbor and Avalon, but they seem quiet, so I thought we should add Sea Isle City for more activity," I explained.

"You mean Island," he corrected.

"No, I'm pretty sure it's Isle," I responded.

"What are you, British all of a sudden?" he said, still convinced I was saying it wrong.

"What?" I asked.

"Do you want a spot of tea when you visit the Isle, Governor?" he said in a Jamaican-Swedish accent.

"Here, look at the brochure," I said, handing him proof that it was *isle*, not *island*.

"Then," he decided, "the whole town must be British."

"Yeah, that's what it is," I pretended to agree.

"So, who's taking us?" he asked.

"I'm not sure," I answered. "My dad is off tomorrow, but I don't know if he'll be in the mood."

"What's better for a bad mood than the beach?" he asked.

While the beach could definitely cure my dad's *bad mood*, T-Bone had a way of curing my dad's *good moods* and I wasn't sure if it would be a good idea. When I asked my mom she said she thought it would be fine.

When I asked my dad, he actually sounded excited to go, even with T-Bone being there. I figured he must have really needed a day away from work. Too bad he missed the Wildwood trip; he would have loved free beaches.

That night, T-Bone and his gear slept over. We drove our normal route, 206 South to the Atlantic City Expressway to the Garden State Parkway. We had read that Stone Harbor and Avalon were located on an island called Seven Mile Beach, with Stone Harbor occupying the southern half and Avalon occupying the northern half.

"Think all of the houses are made of stone?" asked T-Bone as we got closer.

"What?" I asked.

"You know," he began, "stone…harbor."

"No," I answered, not really knowing why, but having a pretty good feeling I was right.

"Then what's their story?" he asked.

"I could answer that one," said my dad. "I read over some of your brochures last night. The first purchaser of what was considered Seven Mile Beach paid $380.00, which was an incredible deal. In fact, today there are roughly 3,000 properties worth over one billion dollars combined."

"That's a lot of zeroes," I added.

"Definitely," my dad agreed. "And that's really impressive since it's only three to four blocks wide."

"Do they have anything besides houses?" asked T-Bone.

"Well, there's that thing called the beach," laughed my dad, "and they have restaurants, shops, water sports, golf, and many other outside activities."

"Why don't they have a boardwalk or a water park?" I wondered.

"You have to realize that not every beach town is a beach resort," my dad explained. "Some towns were designed to encourage visitors and they provide lots of things that motivate people to visit. Other towns are more like neighborhoods that just happen to be by the beach and they prefer life without crowds and chaos."

"Okay," T-Bone said after a few seconds of noticeable thought, "where do the people who live in beach neighborhoods go for boardwalks?"

"I don't know," shrugged my dad. "I guess they go to the closest boardwalk or their favorite boardwalk like everybody else. You know they are allowed to leave."

"Oh," T-Bone nodded while turning red, "I guess I forgot they can go to other beaches, too."

We drove through Stone Harbor and it was a pretty cool town. The houses were really nice and the downtown area was filled with people. We walked around for a little while, took some video, and then headed to Avalon.

When we did our research we learned that Avalon did have a half-mile boardwalk, the kind for walking, not playing games of chance or grabbing a sausage sandwich. Avalon, to our surprise, had an arcade, ice cream shop and a place called Pirate Island mini-golf. It was a great course with waterfalls, caves, and animated pirates. We talked my dad into a quick game, although with T-Bone there's really no such thing. He took forever to line up each shot and even checked for wind every time he approached the ball. My dad compared him to a TV character named Ed Norton, from a show called the *Honeymooners*. This wasn't the first time he compared T-Bone to Ed Norton, so I made a note to borrow my grandfather's DVD and check it out.

We finally finished our game and grabbed some lunch at a place called Nemo's. The food was delicious and it was surprising how hungry one round of mini-golf made us. There was something about this place that made me feel at home and then I read something that cleared up the mystery. Just like me, the owners were from Philadelphia. They now owned two restaurants, one in Stone Harbor and the other here in Avalon. Before we left we complimented them on the food and talked a little Philly. It probably would have been more impressive if we met farther away, like in New Mexico. Apparently, Philadelphians in Avalon is not very unusual.

Right before we left, we noticed a large crowd gathering and laughing. As we crossed the street to investigate, we could see a man juggling away. In addition to that, we realized we were standing in front of Buccaneer Ice Cream and Candies.

"You know," said T-Bone, "a few minutes ago, I was stuffed from Nemo's, but now…"

"Let me guess," I interrupted, "now you're in the mood for ice cream or candy?"

"No," T-Bone corrected, "I'm in the mood for ice cream *and* candy!"

"Well," said my dad, who has been known to have quite a sweet tooth, "we should support the businesses."

It was a good call and we were content and happy as we left Avalon with a bag of candy and headed for Sea Isle City. So far, every beach we had visited had its own unique personality and we were curious to see if that was true for our next stop. The trip to Sea Isle was really quick and we videotaped the drive over.

"You know what's cool?" I asked.

"What's that?" said my dad.

"You can stay in one shore town and still visit other shore towns pretty easily," I replied.

"That's true," said T-Bone, "but the hard part is deciding where to stay."

"It's interesting," my dad began, "that so many families visit the same shore every year and never really explore the other shores. It's great to have a favorite, but it's nice to sample other places, also."

"You mean some kids spend their whole childhood at one beach?" I asked.

"Well, some kids never get to experience the shore at all and of those that do, I would guess that many stick to the same areas," he said.

"That's kind of like eating plain pizza all of your life and never trying a different topping," said T-Bone with an analogy that actually worked; possibly his first.

"That's a good comparison," noted my dad.

"Yeah, it's like eating your favorite ice cream all of the time and never trying another flavor," T-Bone tried again.

"True," my dad agreed once more.

"It's like…" T-Bone tried to whip up a third analogy.

"It's like we get it," I interrupted. "Try different beaches, try different pizzas."

"And different ice cream," T-Bone added with a goofy smile.

Our next stop was Sea Isle City. It was definitely more of a resort town than Stone Harbor and Avalon. Charles K. Landis founded the town in the 1800s to re-create the canals of Venice, Italy. I noticed another Pirate Island mini-golf and T-Bone mentioned he saw one in Stone Harbor, also. I decided to come back and try all three, knowing that pirate history was something T-Bone could never resist.

There was a promenade along the beach, as well as many shops and restaurants. It was really hot, so we broke our tradition and headed straight to the beach. The ocean was filled with bobbing heads, laughing and playing. The beach was covered with sand castles and sea shells and we couldn't wait to touch the water.

We stayed in the water so long, my fingers had shriveled up like little prunes. We decided to try DeNunzio's Brick Oven Pizza and we knew we made the right choice. After dinner we loaded up the car and decided to check out the shops and hunt down an ice cream cone. That was the nice part about evenings at the shore; the sun was fading and it was much more comfortable to walk around.

We ended up at Scoop Daddy's and even though there was a long line, it was worth it. And T-Bone loved the history of it...it was located on *Landis Avenue*.

Chapter Six
Atlantic City to
Ocean City

With each day trip, I found myself more amazed by this little state I once dreaded. New Jersey really did have everything and I found myself annoyed every time I heard someone make fun of it. I wondered if they actually spent any time here or if it was just a habit. Before I could ponder that thought any further, T-Bone was walking in my room.

"Hey, I have some good news," he announced. "I signed us up for the Debate Club."

"You what?" I asked, not sure of what I had just heard.

"I signed us up for the Summer Debate Club at the library," he proudly answered.

"Why did you sign up?" I asked. "And even more importantly, why did you sign me up?"

"I don't know," he shrugged. "It sounded like a really good time."

"A good time?" I sighed. "You know I'm not a great speaker."

"Exactly," he explained. "This will help sharpen your speaking skills. You know, I can't keep carrying us."

"You're kidding, aren't you?" I said, hoping this was a joke.

"No. That new librarian, Miss Albert, told me about it and she said it would be a lot of fun."

"Fun?" I laughed. "I hate public speaking. Remember when we were collecting the stickers at Wrangler Rays? I was a horrible at speaking to strangers."

"I know," he smiled. "You were so bad that one man thought you were on drugs."

"Exactly," I insisted. "My tongue gets tied and my face gets hot. Why would you do this without asking me? And why would you want to do it?"

"I like to talk. Plus, the only other choices were chess, painting, knitting, or drawing."

"I would have picked any of those except, maybe knitting," I shot back. "So why didn't you join by yourself?"

"Because you're the one who needs help," he answered. "Anyway, you'll be fine. She said you just pick a position, clearly explain your position, and then support why you feel that way. Piece of cake."

I couldn't believe he signed me up for Debate Club. For T-Bone, talking to strangers was second nature. He could talk to anyone about anything; me, on the other hand, not so much. The thought of debating someone about anything made me nauseous.

"I also have another reason," he confidently nodded. "Since we're Great Allies of History, *w*ell, at least I am, we can talk about New Jersey."

"You know," I explained, "they don't let you just go up and ramble on about anything you'd like. They give you a topic."

"I know that," he laughed. "But I haven't met a topic yet that I can't work New Jersey into. Try me."

"Okay," I said, accepting the challenge. "Taxes."

"Easy," he began. "Taxes are a necessary fact of life to pay for the services we all enjoy. Tax dollars keep New Jersey's amazing beaches clean and support our many historic landmarks, 36 state parks, and 11 state forests as well as our vast highway system that allows us to visit these wonderful places."

"Not bad," I said, shocked that he came up with such a good argument for something everyone hates. "But what if you had to debate against taxes?"

"Oh, you mean an anti-tax argument?" he smirked. "No problem. Sure, everyone hates taxes, but complaining about them is not the answer. A state like New Jersey should invest more money in travel and tourism so we can collect more money from visitors and lower the tax rates."

Wow, I thought. He must fall asleep listening to the news. How did he know all of this? There was no way I could do that, especially in front of people. What the heck did his family talk about at the dinner table?

"Don't worry," he said. "Our first meeting isn't until next week."

"Great," I mumbled, wondering how I could get out of this. I decided to change the subject by handing him some research for our next trip.

"Cool," he said, as he looked over the brochures. "Ocean City is great. I went there when I was younger. And we went to Margate and Atlantic City with your parents before."

"Yeah, I know," I said, "but last time we were the tourists, this time we're the almost *Official Ambassadors*."

We spent a few hours plotting where we should go and in what order. Having learned how different each beach town really was, it was always exciting to see them firsthand. As we checked out Ocean City's website we learned it was selected Best Beach and Best Beach for Daytrippers in New Jersey many times.

"Hey, look at this," T-Bone pointed to a web page. "Ocean City's one of the top ten surf towns in the country."

"And?" I asked.

"And I can get my surf groove on there," he nodded confidently, as if he could stand up on a boogie board for more than six seconds.

"You might want to learn how to get a boogie board groove first," I laughed.

My grandfather already volunteered for this trip, as he said it was one of his favorite places to bring his family. He suggested we go on Thursday because that was Family Night in Ocean City. They have bands, barbershop quartets, face painting, yo-yo demonstrations and many other things for families. He also suggested we change our routine and start in Atlantic City, then Margate, then finishing the night on the Ocean City boardwalk.

Thursday morning we left very early, after we picked up T-Bone and his usual gear, of course. We were pretty used to the route, except when we got to the end of Route 206 in Hammonton we didn't go to the Atlantic City Expressway. Instead, my grandfather wanted to show us a new route. We made a left onto Route 30 and went in via Absecon. It was nice to see towns as opposed to strictly highway and I took some video from the car.

As we neared Atlantic City, we could see the massive casinos and hotels in the distance. It was really early, so we didn't hit much traffic and luckily the original forecast of showers had already changed three times. The sun was shining and there wasn't a cloud in the sky.

"Look how big it is," T-Bone remarked. "There must be a million people there."

"Actually," said my grandfather, "in the off season, Atlantic City's population is about 40,000 people. More people work in the casinos than live here. But each year over 37 million people visit the city."

"Wow, that's a lot of visitors," I noted. "I guess they all come for the casinos?"

"Many come for the casinos, but Atlantic City is a great seaside resort and they've been re-inventing themselves to cater to families, too," my grandfather explained. "There's much more to Atlantic City than casinos."

We actually learned all about that when we did our research. We decided our first stop would be the Absecon Lighthouse, or Abby, as the locals called her. It was a tall white tower with a large reconstructed Keeper's House at the bottom, now the Visitor's Center, museum and gift shop. Abby is the tallest lighthouse in New Jersey and third tallest in the country at 150 feet. Opened in 1857 at a cost of about $52,000, visitors are invited to climb the 228 steps and get a great view of the area.

It was such a clear day that once we reached the top, it felt like we could see forever. The walk down was much easier and we spent some time checking out the museum. There was a glass case that even contained real items from the Titanic. Of course T-Bone introduced himself to everyone who worked there or happened to be within shouting distance. One family, thinking he must be famous, even had a few pictures taken with him. This is why *he* should be on the debate team, I thought.

When we finished taking our videos we headed over to the Atlantic City Aquarium. I knew it was much smaller than the Camden Aquarium and I was curious to see what they had. It was a nice surprise. While it wasn't a place we would spend the whole day, it was good to include in a day trip itinerary. Inexpensive, close to everything, right on the marina, and they had some really nice tanks and exhibits.

"Hey, get a picture of me," T-Bone said, pointing to a clown fish in the tank. "I'm finding Nemo!"

"Very clever," I shook my head. "Look at those eels behind you."

I laughed when T-Bone jumped, clearly forgetting they were in a tank. They were really ugly, though, and reminded me of the eels from my sister's mermaid movie. When we went upstairs we saw the touch tank where we could pet the stingrays. While I rolled up my sleeve, T-Bone stood a fair distance away.

"How are you gonna pet them from there?" I asked.

"I'm not," he shook his head. "No, thanks."

"Really?" I said, not noticing how uncomfortable he looked. "They're not scary. If anything, they're probably dizzy; you know, they swim in a circle all day."

"I came in with ten fingers and that's how I plan to leave," he announced as two little boys pushed him out of the way to stick their arms in the tank.

"They aren't scary," one boy said to T-Bone. "They want to be your friend. See, just be brave."

"See," I said. "They want to be your friend."

"I have plenty of friends," he responded.

"He's ascared," said the smaller boy. "That big boy is ascared."

The kids were right. T-Bone seemed terrified of the stingrays. Maybe it was the name, maybe it was the pointy tail. Whatever it was, I thought it was pretty funny and made sure I got some video. I decided not to tell him that there were also small sharks in the touch tank.

Before we left, we caught the Dive and Dine Show, where a diver goes in the 25,000 gallon "Fish of the Mid-Atlantic" tank, hand-feeding and interacting with rays, sharks, and other fish who can clearly hold their own in that tank. T-Bone seemed much happier watching someone else interacting with the rays and sharks.

Our next stop was the boardwalk; more specifically, the first boardwalk in the world. It was built in 1870 and was six miles long. We parked on New York Avenue, pretty close to Ripley's Believe It or Not. I had seen the shows on television and I really wanted to be amazed. This place did not disappoint; it was huge inside. I would have never guessed from the boardwalk just how big it really was. The exhibits were so unique and very strange. I decided to stop trying to tape everything and just enjoy it. Plus, we would have run out of space on the camera.

"Hey, am I almost as tall as the tallest man?" T-Bone asked as he measured himself.

"Yeah, you're just about there," I laughed.

"Watch out," I warned T-Bone as he was about to walk in front of a man taking a picture.

"Sorry," T-Bone apologized to the man and then apologized to the woman whose picture was being taken.

Neither one answered and we stood there for a few seconds waiting for them to finish. After about 20 seconds, we both realized they were statues.

"Wow, Ripley got us good, didn't he?" T-Bone laughed.

I just shook my head. I couldn't believe we stopped for statues. I couldn't believe T-Bone apologized to both of them. I really couldn't believe we stood there and waited for them to respond or finish taking their picture. After that, I was on alert. We saw one amazing thing after another and even Ripley himself talking to us. I knew it had to be a video, but it looked so real. Even my grandfather was checking out every item and laughing to himself.

"This is definitely a great place to send families," I said as we met by the exit. "There were so many great things, I'm not sure what my favorite would be."

"I know what you mean," said my grandfather. "It's all so unbelievable."

"Not me," said T-Bone, "my favorite item was the banana the little girl in Italy sent to her aunt in Connecticut with the words *I Love You* written on it. Imagine mailing a banana all the way from Italy. Think she ate it?"

"I don't know if she ate it, but I think I know why you picked a banana as your favorite," I laughed. "Look at the clock; it's almost lunchtime."

"You know, you may be on to something," he agreed. "Lunch, anyone?"

We decided to try one of my grandfather's favorite spots, the White House. It was the equivalent of a Pat's or Geno's cheesesteaks in Philadelphia. There was a long line, but every person who came out was raving about how good the food was. It was a good call. The sandwiches were awesome and we got to eat in an authentic landmark.

After lunch, my grandfather drove by a mural of Atlantic City in the old days. It showed old-fashioned cars, clothes, and even fire trucks. My grandfather said the picture really moved him and in a way, I kind of got it.

Re-energized, we headed to Margate to visit our old friends and get some video footage of Lucy the Elephant with a *Kid Stuff* coupon in hand. I wasn't sure why, but seeing that giant elephant the second time was as exciting as it was the first. It was probably the fact that you don't get to go inside a sixty-five foot pachyderm every day. Having been there before, now I would pay a lot more attention to the details.

We entered the door through her hind leg and started filming. I tried to get a good shot of Lucy's original rib and the exact color on the wall which was that exact color of an elephant's stomach, gastric pink. When we climbed the stairs to get to the riding basket on her back, I took a long look through Lucy's eye. I imagined all of the things she's seen over the years. Just the way clothing and cars had changed was amazing. From the basket, I shot some video, showing the families who visit the website what they could be seeing if they were here.

We thanked our old friends for keeping Lucy going and they thanked us. They were grateful that we had included Lucy in our reports and that more families were now visiting her. I started to feel like T-Bone did when Anne called him a *Great Ally of History.*

"You boys ready to head to Ocean City or are you too tired?" my grandfather asked.

"Too tired? Who, us?" asked T-Bone.

"I heard you get a little tired sometimes," he laughed.

When T-Bone realized my mom must have told him how tired we were in Wildwood, he laughed.

"In our defense," he explained, "Mrs. A. is like a machine. I've never seen anyone have so much energy."

"That's what happens when you spend years chasing after four kids," he smiled.

"And that's exactly why we don't offer babysitting as one of our odd jobs," T-Bone agreed.

Since we were already at the shore, the ride to Ocean City wasn't long at all. It took about a half hour and I taped the scenery along the way. Ocean City reminded me most of Wildwood, with a huge boardwalk and eight miles of white-sand beaches. It also had tons of stores, restaurants, and activities in the neighborhoods off the boardwalk. I could see why families loved it.

I thought we would wait until later to go to the beach, but my grandfather suggested we go now so we would have enough time on the boardwalk later. It was a good call. The day had grown very hot and relaxing by the ocean was definitely a good plan. It was really crowded, but not in a bad way. It looked more like one of those postcards with wall-to-wall umbrellas. By the time I set up the umbrella and the chair for my grandfather, T-Bone was already in the water.

"Don't you want your boogie board?" I hollered to him.

"How can you be bored?" he hollered back.

"No, boogie board!" I tried once more.

"I don't know," he yelled back. "Read a book if you're bored."

"Forget it," I gave up.

"Take a nap if you read it," he responded.

I looked at my grandfather and he just shook his head and rolled his eyes. I sat in the sand for a moment and decided to ask my grandfather about my dad. I wondered if he knew about his job.

"Yes, your dad told me what was going on," he said. "I think he'll be okay, though."

"What does okay mean?" I asked. "Do you think he'll lose his job?"

"I think if a new company buys his store that there will be changes, but that doesn't mean they won't keep your dad," he explained. "I wouldn't worry about it. He's a very hard worker."

"Don't worry?" I asked. "If he loses his job, how will he pay for our house? And if he can't pay for the house we have now, we won't be able to buy a new one. Then we might have to move in with you and I'll have to leave New Jersey."

My grandfather smiled, "There was a time where you would have liked nothing more than to move back to Philly with your old grandparents."

"Yeah, but that was before," my voice trailed off.

"Listen, Nicky, I'll give you the same advice I always

gave your dad. Ninety-five percent of the things we worry about never even happen. So don't worry about the things you cannot control. Instead, use your energy to be prepared in case that thing you are fretting about happens, and then move on."

"Is that really what you do?" I asked.

"Now it is," he nodded. "I wish I could say that I followed that advice when I was younger. But with these creaky old bones and gray hair comes something very valuable…"

"Social Security?" said T-Bone, as he sat down on a dry boogie board.

"No," my grandfather laughed at T-Bone's impeccable timing. "As you get older, you see life differently, less complicated. You wonder why you worried so much."

"I guess," I said, not sure if I could really just turn off the worrying.

"Are you boys ready to dry off, find some dinner and walk the boards?" my grandfather suggested. "There's a great Italian place, it's been here since the 1950s, for take-out. I can't think of the name."

"Is memory loss another thing that comes with the creaky bones and gray hair?" laughed T-Bone.

"I think you're referring to Voltaco's over on West Street," said a woman in the chair next to us. "Sorry to overhear you, but it drives me crazy when I forget names, too."

"That's right, Voltacos," my grandfather smiled. "Thank you. I haven't been here for a while and wasn't sure if they were still here."

"Oh, they're still here all right," she said. "They've become part of Ocean City's history."

"That's great," said T-Bone. "I'm T-Bone and this is Nicky. We're *Great Allies of History*."

"Hi, I'm Patti," she said, slightly confused. "I hope you're sticking around for Family Night tonight."

"Definitely," said T-Bone. "Do you have any other tips? We're New Jersey's *Almost Official Junior Ambassadors* and we're doing research."

"If you're *almost* ambassadors, I should be asking *you* for advice," she laughed. "And, by the way, how do *I* get one of those jobs?"

"I think we have the only ones," T-Bone answered as if she were serious.

"Too bad," she nodded. "Well, you should go to Playland for the rides, get some Johnson's popcorn and then some

Kohr's ice cream. On Pier 9 they have go-karts and Seaport Village Mini-Golf with a replica of Ocean City's historic shipwreck, 'The Sindia' and a fishing village."

"Sounds kind of like the historic mini-golf Mayor Jim wants to do in Burlington City," T-Bone remembered. "I definitely want to try that."

"There's live music, too," she added. "And if you're here in the morning, we always get breakfast at the Chatterbox, kids absolutely love this place. You'll really enjoy it, they've been here over 65 years."

"Food and history are my favorite things," said T-Bone. "Thanks for your help."

"You're very welcome," she said.

Before we turned back around, we heard two familiar little voices.

"Mom-Mom, that's the big boy who was afraid of the touch tank," said the older boy.

"Yeah, he's a scaredy baby," said the smaller one.

T-Bone turned red. Who would have thought that we'd run into the same little boys from the aquarium and that they'd remember T-Bone.

"That's not very nice," Patti scolded her grandkids.

"It's okay," I laughed. "They saw us earlier when my friend was afraid to put his hand in the touch tank."

"Oh," she laughed. "Now, Liam and Conor, tell the boy you were only joking."

"We were only joking, scaredy baby," they said in unison.

"I like these kids," my grandfather laughed.

We left the beach and got some sandwiches at Voltaco's. They were delicious, just like I imagined they would be. The boardwalk was awesome at night: salt air, bright lights, live music, rides, and great food. We rode the go-karts, played mini-golf, and rode the rides. We even managed to get the ice cream and popcorn. It was really late and hard to believe we did so much in one day.

"What do you think?" I asked T-Bone. "Should we make this one day trip or split it into two day trips?"

"Well, I guess if you only have one day, no little kids, and lots of energy, one day is fine," said T-Bone. "Otherwise, you could spend a whole day in Atlantic City/Margate and a whole day in Ocean City."

"Spend the day?" my grandfather laughed. "Boys, you could spend the whole summer at either place and not be bored."

"There's that wisdom again," T-Bone laughed.

Chapter Seven
Long Beach Island

The day after our Atlantic City to Ocean City trip we were exhausted. I knew we should do a couple of odd jobs or at least download our videos and upload them for Billy, but I was exhausted. We got in so late that my grandfather and T-Bone ended up sleeping over. I don't know what time my grandfather woke up, but T-Bone and I slept until my sisters woke us up for lunch.

"Well, look who decided to join us," my mom winked at my sisters.

"Yeah, look who decided to join us," Maggie repeated.

"Yeah, wook it us," Emma tried and just missed.

"Good morning," T-Bone and I said at the same time.

"So what's on your agenda today?" my mom asked.

"Nothing at all," I mumbled.

"Debate Club practice," T-Bone smiled.

"What?" my mom and I said together.

"Yeah, today is the first Debate Club meeting. It's gonna be awesome."

How, I wondered, could he possibly be so energetic and enthusiastic about anything this morning, especially debating? My mom looked totally confused since I had forgotten to tell her about it. My only hope was if she put her foot down and told him I was absolutely not allowed to debate. Ever.

"Very cool," she said. "I had no idea the town library offered clubs like that."

"They have a whole list of them on the internet," said T-Bone. "You should check it out, except you probably don't need a debate club."

"Why's that?" asked my mom, looking confused.

"Because my dad says no married woman needs lessons on how to win an argument," T-Bone smiled.

"That's right," my mom smiled. "Don't you forget it."

We rode our bikes to the library and when we showed up there were stations set up for each club. There were six girls at the knitting station, eight kids at the chess station, a dozen kids at the painting and drawing stations, and then there was the Debate Club. Standing behind the sign was one very enthusiastic librarian and us. Are you kidding me, I thought.

"Hello, Tommy," said Miss Albert. "This must be Nicky."

"Hi," I said, not making eye contact and wondering about the easiest way to get to my bike.

"Well, Nicky, if you want to be a greater debater, you'll need to project that voice," she smiled.

"That's what I've been telling him," T-Bone agreed.

Okay, I thought, there has to be an emergency exit somewhere and this has to qualify as an emergency.

"So, let's go to the conference room and we can get started," she began.

She explained her theory on a great debate: a calm, thoughtful discussion, free of emotion, selecting the right arguments, and listening carefully to your opponent's responses. It all sounded easy enough, but I had some concerns. First of all, I felt like the odd man out, as they both seemed very comfortable speaking in front of others.

Second, as painful as it was to admit, there was no way I could debate T-Bone and win. I didn't even know if I could keep a straight face.

We discussed the rules, she gave us some tips and then handed us the first topic. I was hoping it was something easy. Instead it was confusing: Chores for kids, pro or con. She balled up two pieces of paper and told us each to pick one. I picked pro-chores. I wondered if my mom was behind this as I would have to defend kids doing chores.

As we walked outside to the bike rack, T-Bone was pumped. "This is awesome," he gushed. "I can't wait to come back next week."

"Yeah, I'm counting the minutes," I said as I started pedaling.

When we returned to my house, we started researching our next day trip, Long Beach Island. We had been there with my parents before, but this time we needed to be thorough. Before I could ask anyone to take us, my mom said the whole family would go to LBI together. I was excited because I remembered the fun we had last time.

As usual, we started out early, and once again, T-Bone and his gear stayed over the night before. We piled into the van and finally took another route, Route 70 to the Route 72 circle. It seemed easy enough, but 72 was a long road. LBI only has one bridge to the mainland, so on summer weekends it got really crowded. We left early enough to miss most of the morning traffic and even though it was a cloudy start, the forecast called for sunshine.

"Okay, guys," my dad announced, "we're approaching the causeway."

"The what?" asked Timmy.

"The causeway is the bridge that takes us onto the island," my dad explained.

"We're going to an island?" asked T-Bone. "Cool, I thought we were just going to the beach."

"We're going to both," my mom laughed. "Many of New Jersey's beaches are on barrier islands."

"I don't get it," I said. "Is the island still part of New Jersey even if it's only connected by a bridge?"

"Of course it is," my dad laughed. "Atlantic City is actually on Absecon Island and Ocean City is a barrier island. New Jersey has several islands."

"So we're like Hawaii?" asked Timmy.

"That's kind of a stretch," said my mom. "Hawaii is a group of islands in the Pacific."

"And they have volcanoes," added T-Bone.

"So which way are we going?" I asked as we came to the end of the causeway. "Right or left?"

"Well, since you wanted to check out the Barnegat Lighthouse, I thought we'd do that first," said my mom as my dad headed north to Barnegat Light.

When we got on the island we were in a town called Ship Bottom. There were restaurants, stores, and plenty of houses. My mom said many of the houses were rentals that were usually rented by the week or the season.

"You mean we could live here for the summer?" asked T-Bone.

"You could," my dad laughed. "In fact, I'll help you pick one out."

"Come on, Mr. A., who are you kidding? You'd miss me too much," replied T-Bone.

We continued on The Boulevard to Surf City when my dad parked the car. We all looked out the windows for a lighthouse, but couldn't find one. Instead, my parents were taking us to Scojo's Restaurant.

"Hey, didn't they have a Scojo's at the Tuckerton Seaport?" I remembered.

"Very good," my mom said. "The same family owns them both."

"How do you know that?" asked T-Bone.

"You know, you're not the only one that can surf the web," said my dad.

It was still really early and it looked like the sun was trying hard to come out. While everyone walked inside, I took a few minutes to tape The Boulevard and the restaurant. The food was great and I think everyone had Belgium waffles with strawberries and whipped cream. I never ordered it before, but the two ladies next to us ordered that and it looked delicious. As we headed out, our waitress told us to check out the Interpretive Center at the Barnegat Lighthouse.

After a few minutes we were already in the next town, Surf City, which T-Bone decided was his kind of town. I found it funny that, in his mind, he really considered himself to be a surfer. I noticed Bill Burr's Flamingo Golf and decided to talk my dad into playing an early round. Having my sisters along, I was afraid to put anything important off for later in the day in case one of them had a meltdown.

We continued our drive and soon entered the town of Harvey Cedars. By the time we hit Loveladies, which sounded as manly as living on Dandelion Court, I was wondering if the island ever ended. Once we left Surf

City, the whole atmosphere changed and it seemed much quieter with mostly houses. It was only about nine miles from the causeway to the north end of the island, but when you're excited, that can feel like a lifetime.

As we approached the Barnegat Lighthouse, I was really impressed. It was close to the water, how I imagined all lighthouses would be. Like Abby, this one was tower-style and people called it Old Barney. It was first lit in 1859, making it two years younger than Abby. The price to climb to the top made my dad really happy; adults cost $1.00 and kids under 12 were free.

We stopped by the Interpretive Center first and learned the history of the lighthouse, the shipwrecks, and the changing nature of the coastline. My favorite part was the old pictures that created a timeline of the lighthouse. I imagined it must have been very lonely to be the keeper here, especially in the winter. This end of the island was much different than the middle; there were even fewer houses and fewer people.

My dad, Timmy, T-Bone, and I all climbed to the top while my mom played outside with my sisters. From the top, I got some great video of the 18-mile Long Beach Island to the south, Island Beach State Park across the bay, and Barnegat Bay to the West.

When we returned to ground level, we walked on a path along the coast. Water was crashing against the wall and the sun was now shining. A man inside told us about some great trails and my dad said we could come back without my sisters one day and check them out. Before heading back to Surf City, we stopped by the Barnegat Lighthouse Museum. The museum was maintained by the Historical Society and the Edith Duff Gwinn Garden was maintained by the Garden Club of Long Beach. Since they were only open in the afternoon, we checked out the garden and then I gave a little tour from what I had read.

"This building used to be the elementary school for Barnegat Light until 1951 and there were railroad tracks right out front," I explained. "Girls went in on the left and boys went in on the right."

"Are you sure you read it right?" asked T-Bone. "I don't see any train tracks."

"Actually, before the causeway, in the late 1800s, the train was the only way on the island, other than by boat. Eventually, the train bridge was destroyed by a major storm."

"So they built the causeway?" asked Timmy.

"No, they had a low-level, two-lane auto-bridge and then, in the 1950s, they built the causeway."

"It's hard to believe that a storm could destroy a whole train bridge," said T-Bone.

"Boys, weather has split this island in two and even in smaller pieces, leveled houses and hotels, and almost destroyed the whole island," my mom explained.

"Then maybe we should get going," said T-Bone, heading to the car.

"Relax," said my mom, "those things happened before technology gave us up-to-the-minute weather forecasts, amazing communications abilities, and evacuation routes and procedures. We're fine."

"Plus, it's sunny today," my dad said as he rolled his eyes.

"Good point," said T-Bone.

About twenty minutes later we were on our way back to Surf City. My dad agreed that we should golf before we hit the beach and he pulled up in front of Bill Burr's Flamingo Golf. While there were many great mini-golf courses on the island, my grandmother told me this was her favorite. Every week they even had a tournament. When we approached the booth, T-Bone introduced himself to the man inside. Before I knew it, they were in the middle of a deep conversation.

"You picked a great course," said T-Bone. "This one has history; Bill Burr started it in the 1950s."

"Was that Bill Burr?" I asked, referring to the man at the cash register.

"No, he passed away, but Mrs. Burr is still involved," he told me. "Everybody loved him and he gave everyone a prize, from a dum-dum lollipop to a trophy for a hole-in-one on the last hole."

"So who were you talking to?" I asked.

"Oh, that's Kirk," said T-Bone, as if he knew him his whole life. "He took the reins from Mr. and Mrs. Burr."

Kirk was a nice guy and I was glad that he was taking care of an LBI tradition. We had a great time playing. My mom stayed with my sisters, who shared one club and a pink ball. They stayed one hole behind us serious golfers. Timmy and I each had two holes-in-ones, my dad had one, and T-Bone topped us all. He had four holes-in-ones by the 17th hole. We were all trying to win the trophy on the 18th hole, but one by one we were winning lollipops. T-Bone was on a roll and wanted to go last. My dad looked like he was holding his breath as T-Bone lined up his shot. He gently tapped the ball and we watched, in amazement, as it followed a deliberate path to the hole.

"Yes!" T-Bone yelled and threw his arms in the air. "Did you see that? Did you see that?"

"Didn't need to," my dad said as he shook his head, turned in his club, and took his lollipop.

I went with T-Bone to collect his trophy and while I knew

my dad wasn't jealous of a kid with a trophy, he definitely looked amazed that T-Bone was so lucky. It really was amazing.

My mom suggested we start heading south on the island. We stopped at Dom's Drive-In for some lunch and I think everyone ordered a hot dog and birch beer. The sun started going in and my mom suggested, rather than spending the afternoon on the beach and possibly getting caught in a storm, that we take a beach walk. T-Bone stared at her as if he had no idea what she was saying and I was a little disappointed myself. At the same time, I knew we had spent a lot of time at the shore this summer and we still had several beaches to check out. Just when I thought T-Bone was going to be upset, he sprang into his usual T-Bone mood.

"You know, Mrs. A.," he began. "That's not a bad idea. We can walk by the water, go to Bay Village, after dinner we can go to the Show Place, and then go to Fantasy Island. It's all good."

"That was a quick rebound," my dad laughed. "And it does sound like it will work with the girls, too."

We parked by Fantasy Island in Beach Haven and walked over to the beach. We loved this area last time my parents brought us here. We grabbed a few buckets, a football, and some chairs in case we decided to stay for a little while. We purposely found an area that was wide open. My mom helped my sisters collect shells, while the rest of us started throwing the football around. The sun seemed like it could not make up its mind and I realized my mom probably made the right call. After a while, my parents sat in their chairs at the water's edge.

T-Bone, Timmy, and I played football for a long time. While I managed not to get too sandy, T-Bone and Timmy were covered with sand. They couldn't just catch the football; they had to dive in the sand for each catch. I knew one of the reasons my mom opted to just hang on the beach was to avoid five sandy kids. So much for her plan, I thought.

When we left the beach, we headed over to Bay Village, my mom's favorite place. There were so many shops that she didn't know where to go first. The rest of us occupied my sisters while my mom checked out some of the stores. We played hide and seek with them, which was easy because when Emma had to hide she just covered her eyes. And Maggie talked so much, she was never hard to find. I noticed my mom never came out with any bags and assumed it was because my dad was with us. Turns out she was a much better shopper when he wasn't around.

When everyone started getting hungry, we went to Panzone's. It was a great place for pizza, sandwiches, and pasta and you could eat on the deck outside. When the waitress came over to take our order she made the rookie mistake of starting with T-Bone.

"What can I get you?" she smiled.

"I'm not sure," he said, without looking up. "Do you have lobster?"

"Tommy," my mom said and shook her head.

"Oh, okay, maybe pasta," he said.

The waitress hadn't heard him and asked him if he had said anti-pasta.

"Anti-pasta?" he laughed. "Seriously? I'm pro-pasta."

"Excuse me?" she said, completely confused.

"I think pasta is one of the best foods on earth," he explained. "In fact, I can't imagine why anyone would be against pasta. It gives you energy and it's also very inexpensive. Plus, some of the finest Italian restaurants are right here in New Jersey."

Everyone started looking at each other and I realized T-Bone was about to debate the merits of pasta *and New Jersey* with a teenage waitress.

"I'm sorry," she said, about to lose her patience. "Did you say you want an anti-pasta or not?"

"No," he repeated slowly, as if he was talking to my sisters. "I am pro-pasta. I'll take the rav-i-ol-i."

"Fine," she said, happy to move on to the next person.

When she left, everybody looked at T-Bone.

"What?" he asked.

"This wasn't a debate," I said, shaking my head. "She was asking if you wanted an antipasta; you know, a salad with cheese, salami, tuna, olives."

"Oh, I thought she wanted to know my position on pasta," he smiled.

"What?" asked my dad.

"We joined a debate club and T-Bone thought she wanted to debate him," I said.

"What?" my dad repeated.

"It's okay, Jim," my mom said, making the *I'll tell you later face*. "The boys joined a debate club at the library and I think Tommy is just excited."

"You two joined a debate club?" he laughed. "Nick, you hate speaking in public and Tommy, you, well, let's just say you don't always make sense."

"Thanks," said T-Bone. "I thought it would be fun and Nicky could definitely use practice speaking in front of people."

"So who will you be debating?" asked my mom.

"That's the best part," said T-Bone. "We're debating each other."

"Why?" asked my dad.

"No one else signed up for it," I mumbled.

"Yeah," said T-Bone, shaking his head as he buttered his roll, "some kids just don't know how to have fun."

We finished our dinner and drove over to the Show Place Ice Cream Parlour. There was a line of people waiting to get in, but my mom said they let a lot of people in all at once. I assumed they must have some great ice cream to have a line this long. I peeked inside the window and noticed it looked like an old-fashioned ice cream shop. Fifteen minutes later, the doors opened and we were escorted to our table. We placed our orders and waited for the ice cream. I had no idea that this was ice cream and a real show.

When the ice cream arrived at the table across from us, the waiter announced the little girl's order, had her stand up and started singing about it.

"Wow," said T-Bone, "I should have ordered that."

I'm glad I didn't, I thought to myself. There was no way I wanted to get up and make a fool out of myself. But one table after another, they were serving and singing. I soon realized why each sundae was named after a musical. Since my father didn't like attention, I figured he may wish he hadn't ordered anything at all. It seemed like most of us were safe, since we ordered mint chocolate chip ice cream and whipped cream. T-Bone, on the other hand, ordered the Peter Pan. I was sure he was going to get the spotlight. Unfortunately, our waiter came over wearing a straw hat and announced that our table had four green ice creams. He placed the hat on my dad's head, made us stand up and sing "green ice cream is the thing for me" to the tune of the old show song, *Green Acres*.

After everyone had their ice cream, the Show Place waiters and waitresses performed a singing and dancing show. It was really funny and I couldn't believe they did it over and over again, every night, day after day. Surprisingly, even my dad had a great time, probably because they didn't make him wear the yellow-braids-wig like the guy at the next table.

We headed over to Fantasy Island, went on some rides and played a few games. My Flip Cam was out of space and batteries, my sisters were out of steam, and I was guessing my father was probably out of money. But I got great video and ideas for our reports, so I had everything I needed.

And one thing I didn't…the green ice cream song stuck in my head.

Chapter Eight
Point Pleasant to Seaside

The day after our LBI day trip, I was still singing the green ice cream song. I was waiting for T-Bone to come over so we could organize our videos and write our reports. Since we had so many files to download, my mom thought it would be better to save everything on a memory stick and bring it to the State House. Some of our earlier videos were already downloaded and Billy said they would edit them for us. I started writing the first report and before I was finished, T-Bone had arrived. Unfortunately, he also had a report for the first trip, except his was a song.

"Take a look," he said with a big, goofy smile. "That Show Place gave me an idea."

I started reading and tried not to laugh. I had a feeling he was serious and I didn't want to hurt his feelings.

I'm waking up early to start a new day,
Gonna drive with my friend to sunny Cape May.
I waited all fall, all winter, all spring
To visit a village with the name of Cold Spring.
Then if you ask me what else I'm gonna do
I'll give you three words, it's the Cape May Zoo.
Alligators, zebras, and camels, oh my,
The beach is next, give my boogie board a try.
Last is a place that really can't be beat,
It's an outside mall on Washington Street.

"Wow," I said. "You made a song?"

"Awesome, huh?" he grinned while nodding his head.

I didn't know what to say. New Jersey was really taking us seriously now and T-Bone wanted to sing our reports. There was no way we could give this to Billy, so I tried to quickly think of a good excuse.

"That's a shame we can't use it," I said, pretending to be disappointed.

"What do you mean?" he asked. "Why can't we use it?"

"You want to know why?" I stalled.

"Yeah, I want to know," he said. "Don't you think it's good?"

"Are you kidding?" I said in my most convincing voice.

"It's too good. You should save it in case you're in a band one day. You shouldn't just give it away."

"Really?" he said, giving serious thought to what I had just said. "You think the state won't really appreciate it, right now?"

"I don't even think New Jersey has a band," I blurted out.

"Good point," he agreed. "Maybe I'll write some more and keep them for if I'm ever in a band. Or better yet, maybe one day I'll start a New Jersey band."

"There you go," I said, "that's a much better plan."

By noon, we had just finished writing our last report. Writing so many shore reports at once taught me one thing. In the future we had to write them the next day. After a while, one trip started blending into the next trip and we had to keep double-checking ourselves with the video. My mom came into my room to see if we were ready.

We hopped in the van and headed to Trenton. When we walked in the State House, the security guard recognized us immediately and called Billy.

"Hey, there's our future ambassadors," Billy said as he shook our hands.

"Future?" asked T-Bone.

"Well, the Legislature still has to vote on it, but everyone is very supportive of your work."

"Will that be soon?" I asked.

"We're hoping it's real soon," he smiled. "Just keep up the great work. And, by the way, how are the Flip Cams working out?"

"Great," we both answered.

"Well, I have to run to a meeting," he said, "but let me know when you have more video and reports."

"Will do," I said as we headed out.

"So, are you boys hungry?" asked my mom.

"Are you kidding?" said T-Bone. "I'm always hungry."

We drove from Trenton to Hamilton Township and pulled into a parking lot for a place called Pete's Steakhouse. My mom said they were known for their cheesesteaks, but that everything was delicious. It was big inside and filled with a hungry lunch crowd. We all ordered the Big Pete's steak and fries and we were not disappointed. I read the history of Pete's on the menu. After World War II, Pete Tonti opened a steakhouse on Chambers Street in Trenton and served 7,000 cheesesteaks each day at twenty-five cents each. Now, his son, Rich, and his wife, Gina, run Pete's Steakhouse in Hamilton.

Just as we finished eating, a woman walked over and asked us if everything was okay. It was Gina, Rich's wife. When T-Bone told her about our jobs, she was very impressed.

"You know," she said, "my son, Pete, read about your reports and we've visited Morristown and Wild West City thanks to you boys."

"Really?" asked T-Bone. "Did you have fun?"

"We had a great time," she smiled. "And we're looking forward to following more of your adventures. So keep up the good work."

"We will," we assured her.

It was fantastic to actually meet someone who followed our trips. I wondered how many families were visiting the places in our reports. Billy said many people were, but it didn't sink in until we met Gina and heard about Pete. We hoped we could meet him one day.

When we got home we were more excited than ever to plan our next day trip. We decided to visit the Barnegat Peninsula, including Seaside, Ortley Beach, Lavallette, Normandy Beach, Mantoloking, Bay Head, and Point Pleasant Beach. It sounded like a lot, but the two big resorts were Seaside to the south and Point Pleasant to the north, and we were curious to see what was in between.

A few days later, my grandfather picked us up and we were on our way. He suggested we start at the north end of the peninsula and work our way down so we could start with Jenkinson's Aquarium. We parked behind the boardwalk and walked to the aquarium. There were little kids wearing the same blue t-shirt, so I assumed they were part of a summer camp trip. I was hoping we would run into the little boys we met in Atlantic City.

The aquarium was really nice. They had huge tanks and we were there for the feeding time. They had a touch tank that T-Bone avoided at all costs, however he had no problem walking through the glass tank tunnel. It was outstanding to feel like we were underwater with the fish and sharks and I hoped the glass was really strong. My favorite part, other than the tunnel, was the penguins. It was funny watching them waddle around in their tuxedos.

When we left the aquarium we strolled the boardwalk for a little while. We went to the arcades, played some games, and had lunch at Jenkinson's. When we finished eating, T-Bone wanted to go in the Fun House. I remembered going in a fun house when I was little and getting stuck. There were so many mirrors and glass walls that I didn't know which way to turn and I ended up sitting on the floor and crying. I also remembered my parents getting into an argument and my mom telling my dad that she knew I was too little to go inside.

"We should probably get going," I suggested. "We don't want to run out of time."

"Are you kidding?" asked T-Bone. "I'm the master of fun houses. I was practically born in a fun house. We'll be out in five minutes."

"Fine," I said reluctantly. "Should we go in together?"

"If you feel like you need to follow me, then sure," he said.

"Never mind," I replied, "I'll see you on the other side."

Thankfully, it wasn't as confusing now as when I was five years old. I was careful not to walk into my reflection and hoped T-Bone didn't come out much quicker than me. If he did, I would never hear the end of it. When I reached the exit, I saw my grandfather sitting on a bench.

"Hey, where's T-Bone?" I asked.

"The master's still inside," he laughed.

"Really, he didn't come out yet?" I asked. "I thought for sure he would have beat me out."

"I think he thought that, too," he said.

We waited about ten minutes and finally T-Bone came out with a wad of paper towels up against his face and an older woman leading him out. My grandfather and I just looked at each other.

"What happened to you?" I said, trying not to laugh.

"I zigged when I should have zagged," he replied.

"I think he's a little dizzy," the woman said. "He's not making much sense."

"Don't go by that," my grandfather laughed and thanked the woman. "We've got him from here."

We sat on the bench until his nose stopped bleeding. We were going to go on a few rides, but my grandfather suggested lemonade and skee-ball. I assumed he was trying to find low-impact activities. We stopped in the Magical Carousel Gift Shop, then Lucky's Arcade. We played a couple of wheels, and watched T-Bone win us each a Phillies Jersey with only 12 quarters.

"This kid's like ol'King Midas," my grandfather grinned and shook his head. "Is he *ever* unlucky?"

"Yeah," I laughed, "in the fun house."

We headed back to the car and south on Route 35 toward Bay Head. When we did our research, their website described the town as a country village by the sea, established in the late 1800's. It said there were many things to do nearby, but Bay Head was much quieter than the resort towns. There was shopping, restaurants, bed and breakfasts and hotels, and a yacht club, but it wasn't very *touristy*.

104

"Wow, this place is really fancy," T-Bone said as we passed some pretty big houses.

"I'll say," I agreed. "Hey, look at that house."

"That's like five of my house," T-Bone laughed.

"Too much to clean," my grandfather laughed. "You know they call Bay Head the Hamptons of the Jersey Shore."

"Really?" said T-Bone. "What's the Hamptons?"

"It's a wealthy beach area in Long Island," he explained. "And, no, it's not in New Jersey, it's in New York."

As we continued on Route 35, we entered Mantoloking. As with Bay Head, Mantoloking was not a resort town, but more like a neighborhood by the ocean. I looked at the papers I printed as we rode through the town.

"Hey, Pop, listen to this," I began, "it says if you plan to stay on the beach more than two hours, there are no bathrooms, no food, no shade, and parking is limited. It even says stay close to the water because the upper beach is someone's front yard. How are they going to get tourists to visit like that?"

My grandfather started laughing and reminded us that some towns were designed as resorts and others were residential.

"This reminds me of Stone Harbor and Avalon," I remembered. "They were really nice, but they were like regular towns, too."

"Yeah," T-Bone agreed, "there wasn't a merry-go-round to be found in either place."

By the time we finished our discussion, we were entering Normandy Beach, which was very similar to its neighbors to the north. Lots of nice houses, and they had a yacht club, too. It was a nice ride and I didn't mind checking out the houses and scenery. Even though these towns were mostly houses, I still taped them. Our goal was to show what people would see if they were in the towns we visit, even if they didn't have boardwalks.

Next, we entered Ortley Beach, one beach away from another boardwalk. Ortley Beach had a park, arcade, mini-golf, bike rentals, and even bathrooms by the beach. While looking at fancy houses was good, we were well-rested at this point and ready to have some fun. We checked out the boardwalk, which was actually a walkway made of boards, and stopped to watch the ocean for a few minutes. I got a few more shots and we were ready for our next stop, Seaside Heights.

It was a really short ride and T-Bone said he could smell the food from inside the car. My grandfather told him it was all inside his head.

"I'd rather it all be inside my stomach," he laughed.

We parked in a lot and headed to the boardwalk. There was something really exciting about walking up the ramp. The back side of the boardwalk could be any old street, but once you reached the boards, it was a whole other world. Standing across from the Atlantic Ocean, hearing the waves crash and seagulls squeal while inhaling the smell of pizza, sausage, and cotton candy was one of the things that made the Jersey Shore so Jersey.

"Where to first?" asked my grandfather.

"Round trip on the Sky Ride, to start," announced T-Bone as if he had some sort of schedule. "From up above, I can survey the situation."

"What's to survey?" I asked. "We've been here before."

"As tourists," he reminded me, "not as ambassadors."

So, while my grandfather sat on the bench with a fresh-squeezed lemonade, T-Bone and I took the Flip Cam and rode the Sky Ride.

"This will make some great video from up here," T-Bone observed. "When people watch this they'll all want to come here."

"Hopefully, all of our videos and reports will make people visit all of the places we visited," I added. "After all of our day trips, I can confidently say that New Jersey is the most amazing state in the country."

We left the Sky Ride and tried everything the Casino Pier had to offer; rides like the Go-Karts, Log Flume, Wave Swinger, the Wild Mouse, the arcade and the historic carousel. We remembered meeting Dr. Floyd Moreland, the man who saved the over-one-hundred-year-old carousel from the Burlington Island Amusement Park. When we first met him, we didn't really appreciate the work he did to save something so historical. But having been to the City of Burlington and meeting Mayor Jim made it even more impressive.

We played some of the wheels and as usual, T-Bone won a case of candy, a football, and a Phillies mirror. We checked out the Funtown Pier, which lived up to its name, and then decided to investigate Breakwater Beach, Jenkinson's Water Park. It looked awesome, but we knew we didn't have enough time to try it out…this time. We took some video and decided we'd definitely be back, probably with my Dad and the *Kid Stuff* coupon book.

It was getting late and we decided to grab a snack and then grab our chairs and umbrella. Hitting the beach when everyone else was leaving had become our tradition, and it was nice to have our own thing.

While my grandfather assumed his position under the umbrella, T-Bone and I floated on our boogie boards. We were both too tired to let the ocean toss us around. It was so peaceful I could have fallen asleep on my board until T-Bone started talking.

"So boardwalks, pro or con?" he asked as he bobbed up and down on his board.

"What?" I asked.

"It's a debate," he said, assuming I didn't know what he was doing.

"I get that," I laughed. "But what do you mean with boardwalks, pro or con?"

"Well, we've been to beaches with awesome boardwalks that have rides, games, food stands, and even water parks," he began. "But we've also been to beaches with just walkways made of boards along the beach and some that didn't have any type of boardwalk. So when it comes to boardwalks, are you pro or con?"

"What side are you taking?" I asked.

"Doesn't matter," he confidently replied. "Miss Albert said a skilled debater can argue either side of an argument."

"Isn't that kind of like lying?" I asked. "Not saying what you believe in, just saying what someone wants to hear?"

"No, no, no," he assured me, "it's forcing yourself to see things from different sides. She said it makes you a better speaker and thinker."

"Okay, I'll say con," I began, hoping to see how I measured up by not picking the one I agreed with. "Beaches are natural treasures and boardwalks with rides and games take the attention off of their natural beauty. They also bring large numbers of people that, I don't know, make things louder and more, what's the word, crowded."

"Not bad," he nodded, "especially without any time to prepare."

"Thanks," I said, "your turn."

"All right," said T-Bone, "beaches are natural treasures and boardwalks help bring more people to enjoy them, plus they have bathrooms."

"That's it?" I asked. "Bathrooms?"

"They're important when you need them," he laughed. "Plus, Miss Albert said we shouldn't overdo it and once we've supported our position, we should stop."

"Great," I smiled. "I win."

"How do you figure?" he asked.

"You missed too much," I explained. "Boardwalks bring families together, memories, traditions; I think you underdid it."

"Good critique," T-Bone laughed and rolled off his board.

That was the great thing about him. He never took himself too seriously and really was a good listener. I wondered if I would have reacted the same way if he gave me the same critique.

We ran to our umbrella and dried off. My grandfather had dozed off and woke up as we put on our shirts.

"You boys hungry?" he asked.

"Starving," I said. "How about the Sawmill?"

"I'm pro on that topic," said T-Bone.

"Too bad you won't have anyone to debate," I laughed. "I think you'd have a hard time finding anyone to debate against pizza at the Sawmill."

The atmosphere of the Sawmill was really relaxed and I was looking forward to returning. We ordered one pizza that was not only delicious, but just as I remembered, as big as the table. We ate as much as we could and hardly put a dent in it. Our waitress wrapped up the half that was left over and we were on our way. We decided to hang out longer so we could enjoy the boardwalk all lit up and, of course, find some ice cream. It didn't take long.

"So, did we finish the peninsula?" asked T-Bone.

"Pretty much," I said as I tried to stop the ice cream from melting down the cone. "The only town south of here is Seaside Park, which is mostly houses, and then Island Beach State Park."

My parents had taken us to Island Beach before and, since it was a state park, we knew it would be closed. We took a little more video and decided to call it a day.

"You boys ready to go home?" asked my grandfather.

"I'm pro on that idea," T-Bone yawned.

"No debate here," I agreed. "No debate here."

And with that, we wrapped up yet another exciting and different Jersey Shore adventure.

Chapter Nine
Manasquan to Long Branch

"Hey, Nick," Timmy whispered.

I pretended not to hear him.

"Hey, Nick, Nick, hey, Nick," he continued, "wake up."

This time I not only pretended not to hear him, I also pretended to not realize my hand was pushing his face away. I made a couple of grumbling noises and hoped he would get the picture. He didn't. Instead of going away, he came closer. I could feel his breath on my forehead as he stared at me and I wasn't sure how much longer I could play opossum.

"Nick, Nick, hey, Nick, wake up," he pleaded, "you and T-Bone are going to be on the news."

"What?" I asked. "Is this some kind of a trick to wake me up? Because if it is, I'll…"

"No joke," he insisted. "Hurry up, before you miss it. Hurry!"

"What about T-Bone?" I asked. "Do I have time to call him?"

"No need," said Timmy, as we ran down the stairs, "he's in the kitchen."

"What?" I asked. "T-Bone's here already?"

"Yeah," Timmy answered, as if T-Bone was always here before I woke up. "He's helping Mom make breakfast."

"What?" I asked as I rubbed my eyes and yawned. I was really confused. Was I really going to be on the news? How did I miss the cameras? And was T-Bone really cooking breakfast with my mom?

"Good morning," said T-Bone as he flipped a pancake. "Blueberry or chocolate chip?"

"Really?" I asked. "You want to debate now?"

"No," he laughed, "I'm just trying to figure out what kind of pancake you want. But that wasn't a bad idea. I'll take blueberries; they're healthy, delicious, and they don't make a mess."

114

"I'll take chocolate chip," I grumbled.

"And your reason?" T-Bone prodded.

"Because I'm starving?" I said, ready to eat, not debate. "And what's this about being on the news?"

"Oh, I TVR'd the news," my mom smiled, still unable to remember the abbreviation DVR. "Here, I'll hit play."

I wasn't sure what to expect. It could have been a press conference at the State House with Billy announcing that T-Bone and I were overwhelmingly voted *Official Junior Ambassadors*. Or maybe it was one of the places we wrote about talking about how we saved them from going bankrupt. Or it could have been a family that visited all of the places from our reports and wanted to publicly thank us.

Or…it could have been T-Bone, my grandfather, and I walking down the boardwalk as a weatherman placed the five-day forecast over us. That was it, I thought. Are you kidding me? We were just captured on Channel 6's Accu-Weather Boardwalk Cam and they woke me up? I could barely see my head under the word humidity. These better be good pancakes, I thought.

Everyone was raving about how natural we looked. Of course we looked natural, we were taped on a hidden camera. Something would have been wrong if we didn't look natural.

"From now on, I'm going to smile when I walk," T-Bone announced. "You just never know."

"Really?" I asked. "You're just going to walk around with a big smile slapped on your face."

"Yup," he smiled.

"Just in case there's a camera that you happen to walk in front of and they happen to put that ten-second clip on television again?" I sarcastically tried to prove a point.

"Precisely," he smiled wider and winked.

"Pass the syrup," I said as I shook my head.

"So when's the next trip?" asked my mom. "You guys are on quite a roll."

"We'll start in Manasquan and see how far we get," I answered.

"No end point?" T-Bone observed. "That's very Thomas Jefferson of us."

"You mean Lewis and Clark?" I corrected him.

"No, Thomas Jefferson sent those guys out to explore," he continued.

"Exactly, we're like Lewis and Clark because we're

doing the exploring," I tried to explain. "We're the explorers."

"Au, contraire," he laughed, "aren't we also the guys who are planning the trips and aren't we sending the world out to explore New Jersey? We're Thomas Jefferson."

When he put it that way, he actually had a point, although, I probably could have argued the point that we were a combination of both: exploring everything firsthand and then sending other people.

"So what is a Manasquan?" he asked. "Is that someone's last name? A tribe of Native Americans?"

"You're close," I said. "It's a Native American word. One meaning is Stream of the Island of Squaws."

We grabbed the atlas and headed to the computer. At first glance, it seemed like this section of shore towns was tighter than the other sections we had visited. They were closer together and it seemed like they all had a pretty equal share of the ocean. I was curious to see if they were all alike since they were so close. It was hard to imagine each one could be that close and yet that different.

T-Bone and I took a couple of days to catch up on some odd jobs and go to our debate practices. We stopped by our old friend George's house and moved some things around for him. When we finished, he offered us some lemonade on his front porch.

"You know," he started, "one day you boys may have your own television show."

"Like a cartoon?" asked T-Bone. "I would definitely be Tom, from Tom and Jerry."

"No, I meant like yourselves, on a travel show," George laughed. "Maybe Nicky and T-Bone's New Jersey."

"Things like that don't happen to guys like us," I informed him.

"Did you ever think you'd be New Jersey's *Almost Official Junior Ambassadors*?" George cleverly inquired.

"Honestly," I replied, "I didn't think I'd ever be New Jersey's anything, other than neighbor."

"So, where's the next adventure?" asked George.

"The Island of Squaws," T-Bone answered with a huge smile. "We haven't picked an end town yet; kind of flying by the lick of a promise."

"I think you just mixed your metaphors," I laughed.

"This coming from the guy who mixes pretzels and chocolate," T-Bone shrugged.

"That's normal," I explained. "Sweet and salty actually go together."

"Tommy, I think you meant to say flying by the seat of your pants or planning the trip with a lick and a promise," said George. "Both mean you're being spontaneous."

"Okay," T-Bone agreed, "but I still prefer my pretzels without chocolate."

"Whatever," I quickly tried to steer the conversation back to our next trip, hoping George had some suggestions. "Have you ever been to Manasquan?"

"Actually, I drive to the beach quite often, and not just in the summer," said George. "I find it very relaxing and much more exciting than sitting on a mall bench. I enjoy Manasquan, Sea Girt, Spring Lake, Belmar, Avon-by-the-Sea, and Bradley Beach."

"Any good tips?" asked T-Bone.

"Well, they're all really fine beaches and towns, but I think you should check out the Sea Girt Lighthouse," George suggested.

The next day, my grandfather picked us both up at my house. The northern shores were closer than the southern shores so we didn't need to leave before sunrise. Once again, T-Bone ran the whole way to my house, dragging all of his gear behind him.

"I wasn't sure what we would need," he said, "so I brought a little of everything."

We loaded the car and were on our way. Our first stop was Manasquan and we had a good idea of what it would be like. T-Bone looked at the map and noticed the Manasquan Inlet. He wondered why the inlet was outside and outlets were usually inside. My grandfather almost got snookered into that debate, but thought better of it.

We drove through the town, headed over to the ocean and took some video. I had read that Manasquan had a small year-round population, but like most Jersey Shore towns, the population swelled each summer. This was no exception. Families were walking through the town, kids with buckets were headed to the beach, and an ice cream truck was stirring up excitement.

"I have a bag full of quarters, all ready for the boardwalk games," said T-Bone.

"You know Manasquan doesn't have that kind of a boardwalk, right?" I asked. "It's a promenade along the beach with shops and restaurants. They don't have games."

"None?" he asked.

"Sorry, sport," my grandfather laughed. "But I wouldn't worry too much, I think you'll have a great time."

We took a walk to check out the boardwalk businesses. The town was bustling, but I wondered how hard it must have been to sell things in the winter. I figured maybe some of the stores only opened during the busy season. After all of our trips, I realized that no matter how different the beaches were, they had one thing in common: everyone was always smiling. It was hard to find people frowning at the Jersey Shore. Maybe it was the salt air, the seagulls, or the crashing of the waves; whatever it was, it sure made people relax and enjoy themselves.

After a little while, we headed to Sea Girt. I was excited to check out the lighthouse, especially since it was the house-style variety. I figured T-Bone would be excited to hear about its history, too. It was similar to Manasquan in that it was very residential and wasn't a tourist destination or a resort. It didn't seem like a beach neighborhood, but a neighborhood that happened to be right next to the beach.

We parked by the boardwalk and started filming.

"Where's the lighthouse?" asked T-Bone.

"I don't know," I said, slowly scanning the landscape.

"Maybe we should head over to that house and ask them if they know where it is," suggested T-Bone.

"You mean that house with the tower sticking out of the roof?" I sarcastically asked.

"Yeah, that's the one," he said, totally unaware that he was pointing to the lighthouse.

I wondered if I should let him go in and actually ask for directions. Then I thought about what my father would do in this situation and I sent him inside to ask. He walked right past the sign and disappeared from sight. After about ten minutes, he returned with a big smile.

"Hey, Nick," he began, "you're not gonna believe it, but this *is* the lighthouse!"

"No kidding?" I asked, pretending I really didn't know. "Are you sure?"

"Yeah, I just asked the lady inside," he replied. "Should I go ask her again?"

I thought about it for a moment, looked at my grandfather, and said, "Yeah, go ahead."

Upon his second return, he was confident that we were at the lighthouse. Ironically, my grandfather and I were standing in front of the sign both times.

"So what did you find out?" I asked.

"Well," he began, "In the late 1800s, they needed to light up the long coastline between Sandy Hook and Barnegat Inlet. Congress set aside $20,000.00 to purchase land near the Manasquan Inlet to build a lighthouse. Construction began in 1895. It was finished and first lit up on December 10, 1896. The Sea Girt Lighthouse became the last live-in lighthouse on the Atlantic Coast."

"Are you auditioning for a job here?" I asked, totally in shock that T-Bone memorized all of that information.

"If only," he smiled. "It's not that hard to remember something you're interested in, you know."

He was right. I couldn't remember the state capitals, but I could remember baseball stats without even trying. T-Bone had become such a history buff that sometimes, when he talked about things he had read, it was as if he had been there.

"Ready to go in?" asked my grandfather.

"Absolutely," we said together, and headed to the door.

I decided that if I had been a lighthouse keeper, this is probably the house I would have picked. It was decorated nice and wasn't so far from everything. There was a nice fireplace and bookcases. We learned that the building was once a library and a meeting place and, like many of the historic places we had visited, it was saved by a civic group.

"Could you imagine if they would have let this lighthouse be destroyed?" T-Bone asked in amazement.

"Well, I guess it gets expensive to keep old buildings going," I said, simply acknowledging that it must cost a lot of money.

"What?" he sneered. "What would happen if the Italians and the Greeks didn't value history? There would be no Coliseum, no Ruins. Governments have to save history."

"You have a good point," my grandfather agreed. "I still can't believe you have become one of history's, uh, what's the word?"

"Greatest Allies?" T-Bone smiled.

"Sure," said my grandfather. "But you are right. Today's governments, federal, state, and local, have a real obligation to preserve history. The past is the key to the future and history and the arts must be a priority."

"Or, like they say in the City of Burlington," T-Bone proudly remembered, "the Past is our Present to you."

When they finished debating the merits of history, we followed Ocean Avenue north to Spring Lake. Spring Lake was a resort town, but like Sea Girt, it was quieter than a Wildwood or Seaside. The houses were really nice and the town had two miles of beachfront. Spring Lake had the record for the longest non-commercial boardwalk and my grandfather confirmed that meant a boardwalk with no businesses. It was quiet and I could picture my family riding our bikes along the beach.

We walked along the boardwalk and took some video. I remembered my days living in Philadelphia, when I had no idea what New Jersey had. Then I thought about all of the things people think about the Garden State. After about 45 minutes we returned to the car and headed north toward Belmar.

"Wow, look at all of the umbrellas," T-Bone noticed. "That's awesome."

"This place is hopping," I added.

Belmar had a younger feel and it looked like there were many more visitors. After all these day trips, I was still amazed that each town had its own distinct personality. We checked out the downtown area and even found a skate park. While the boardwalk didn't have businesses, T-Bone was the first to notice they had plenty of bathrooms and there were businesses right across the street. We walked around, took some video and continued north to Avon-by-the-Sea, another small Jersey Shore community.

"Hey, that's a mouthful," T-Bone laughed as we rode past the welcome sign. "My grandmother used to sell Avon; think it's the same company?"

"No," I shook my head, "the town's website said it was named after the famous explorer Lief Ericson's son, Nels Avone."

"No way," said T-Bone. "I've heard of him. Not Nels, but that Lief guy."

"Just think," I observed, "if you stand right here and look only at the ocean, you can see what the explorers saw when they arrived here."

"Poor guys," said T-Bone, "they were probably here before the bathrooms."

"Probably?" I asked in my most sarcastic tone.

"That's true," he said after giving it some thought, "most of these houses probably weren't here either."

"T-Bone," I said while taking a deep breath, "you do realize that when the first explorers came here, there was nothing here; no houses, no restaurants, no stores, no buildings, and…"

"No bathrooms," he completed my sentence.

We stayed for a while and headed to Bradley Beach. I remembered reading that Captain Kidd had buried his treasure in Bradley Beach and that it was never recovered. I figured this was a fact that T-Bone didn't need to know, although with his luck, he'd probably stumble right on it.

Bradley Beach had a nice boardwalk with gazebos every so often. I figured out that the closer we got to Asbury Park, the livelier each town became. While Bradley Beach was small, with only about 5,000 actual residents, each summer about 30,000 people visited. The beach had a concession stand, beach chair and umbrella rentals, and the best part, kids under 13 were free. T-Bone even spotted a sign for miniature golf.

We grabbed a small pre-lunch snack at the concession stand and took some nice videos while we sat on a boardwalk bench.

"I'd like to come back here," said T-Bone.

"I'd like to come back to all of them," I agreed. "It's good to be an ambassador, but we don't always get to stay long enough."

"Well, now that you know what each of these towns offers, you can come back with your parents," said my grandfather.

He had a great point. As ambassadors, we were like scouts, going out and reporting back with everything we saw. But we were still kids and could come back and enjoy each town just like the kids who read our reports. Best of both worlds, I decided.

Our next stop was Ocean Grove. There was a really nice shopping district on the main street, with stores and restaurants. The town was busy and we noticed a huge church and rows of cabins with canvas tents. I never saw anything like this and was curious. In front of the tents were people sitting on makeshift porches with iced tea and books while church music played for the whole town.

My grandfather explained that each summer people flocked to Ocean Grove for religious meetings. Families rented the tents from the church and stayed for the summer. There was even a huge waiting list to get a tent. A nice older lady spoke with us and explained that behind the tent was a cabin with a kitchen, bathroom, living room, and a bedroom. She gave us a brief tour and said this was her parents' cabin, where she spent her summers when she was a young girl. She even told us that when she was a young girl, driving in Ocean Grove was never allowed on Sundays.

We walked on the boardwalk and crossed the border into Asbury Park. I knew it was a famous shore town because my father was a huge Bruce Springsteen fan and I remembered he had a CD called *Greetings from Asbury Park*. My grandfather said Asbury Park was one of the greatest resorts in the country and during its heyday, it was the place to be.

"Then what happened?" asked T-Bone.

"Life happened," said my grandfather. "Everything has peaks and valleys; some more so than others. For a while Asbury Park had lost some of its luster."

"Why didn't people fix it?" T-Bone asked very logically.

"These things happen, and it's usually a combination of reasons," my grandfather explained. "Some towns are more vulnerable when the economy goes downhill."

"I don't know what that means," I admitted, "but I think it looks pretty awesome now."

"Yes," my grandfather smiled, "the good news is Asbury Park has been making a wonderful comeback."

"Look," said T-Bone, pointing to a water playground on the boardwalk. "That's awesome."

I had to admit it was pretty cool. A little farther down was a miniature golf course and I was hoping my grandfather would let us play a round. We stopped at Sicliana's and sat outside. There was almost nothing better than eating on the boardwalk and overlooking the Atlantic Ocean.

"That was great pizza. You boys feel like a round of mini-golf?" asked my grandfather.

"Absolutely," said T-Bone, "but before we do that, I think we should visit the Candyteria."

"The what?" I asked, sure I heard him wrong.

"You didn't see the Candyteria?" he asked. "It looks like the most amazing candy store ever."

He was right. They had everything and as much as I tried not to overdo it, every time I turned around I found another favorite candy. We left the candy store and headed to the mini-golf. The course had yellow plaques that gave some of Asbury Park's music history and we learned just how important it was. From the golf course we could see the Stone Pony where Bruce Springsteen started out and the Convention Center. Adjacent to the Convention Center was the famous Paramount Theater. While every beach was amazing, there was something really special about Asbury Park. I wasn't sure if it was the history and hundreds of famous people who walked the same boards or because it was the beginning of an exciting new page in their history. We stopped by *Hot Sand*, a cool glass studio that let kids, starting at nine years old, blow their own glass. It only took us twenty-minutes and we had each created an amazing ornament.

We said goodbye to Asbury Park and headed north. We drove through the shore towns of Loch Arbor and Deal. I had never heard of either one and I decided the kids who lived in these huge houses were pretty lucky. Not only were the houses enormous, they were right by the ocean on wide tree-lined streets. We were heading to our last stop of the day, Long Branch and I knew T-Bone would love it. Long Branch, along with Cape May, was one of the first shore resorts in the country. It was so famous that many presidents summered in Long Branch and it was even referred to as the Summer Capital.

We pulled into Pier Village. We parked and walked past tall buildings of condominiums surrounded by neatly manicured grass and landscaping. As we neared the boardwalk, we could see shops and restaurants on the bottom of the buildings. We saw Stewart's Root Beer, one of my favorite restaurants, and I immediately started thinking of a frosty root beer and a pork roll and cheese.

"Hey, let's take a walk on the boardwalk," I suggested.

"Nah, let's go on the beach," said T-Bone.

"Trust me," I smiled, "you'll want to see this."

"Do they have a wheel?" he asked.

"No."

"Do they have Whack-A-Mole or the Frog-Bog?"

"No."

"Then why are you so excited?"

"You'll see," I said, as I led them both toward Presidents Park. When we got closer, I could see T-Bone's eyes starting to light up.

"Hey, Nick, look at this," he said. "It's every president who stayed here. It's amazing."

"Long Branch was placed *on the map* in 1869 when President Grant made the city the nation's "Summer Capital," I read from my research notebook, "a tradition followed by Presidents Hayes, Garfield, Arthur, Harrison, McKinley, and Wilson. In the late 1800s Seven Presidents Oceanfront Park was the site of 'The Reservation' that

Long Branch businessman Nate Salsbury built for his Buffalo Bill Wild West Show. Buffalo Bill Cody, Annie Oakley, and Chief Sitting Bull were among the many performers."

There was a statue of President James Garfield and monuments of the other six presidents that spent time in Long Branch. We took some video and checked out the rest of the park. There was a big playground and even a skate park. It was getting close to dinner time and we all decided that we should cool off on the beach.

We grabbed T-Bone's gear from the car and set up by the water. After visiting so many shore towns in one day, it was great to finally feel the water. The crowds that filled the beach when we first arrived had really thinned out.

"This was some day," said my grandfather. "You really did see a number of different beaches, didn't you?"

"I'll say," I agreed.

Later, we headed to Stewart's and feasted on a Jersey original, the *Jersey Burger*; a cheeseburger topped with pork roll, accompanied by fries, onion rings, and a frosted mug of root beer. We stopped by Cake, Bake and Roll, an amazing bakery that even had a sundae bar. We toasted the Jersey Shore and our favorite places of the day. T-Bone picked Long Branch, I picked Asbury Park and my grandfather couldn't decide. He had a good point.

Chapter Ten
Monmouth Beach to Keansburg

It took a few days to recover from our Manasquan-to-Long Branch trip. I never knew how exhausting travel could be and I was looking forward to a day of relaxation. I wasn't sure what I would do, but I knew I wouldn't be doing odd jobs, visiting beaches, or writing reports. It took almost a day to download our latest videos and write our report, and I needed a break.

"Nick, Nick," my brother called out as he entered my room. "Hey, Nick, you wanna play chess?"

"Nope," I answered.

"How about checkers?" he tried again.

"Nope," I answered.

"How about hide and seek?"

"Okay," I said, "you hide and I'll find you."

"Great," he exclaimed and ran out of my room.

Perfect, I thought. T-Bone was shopping with his mom and Timmy would be in his usual hiding spot, the coat closet, for at least the next forty-five minutes. I wasn't sure what I wanted to do first, so I grabbed my baseball glove and started tossing the ball while I thought it over. I thought about riding my bike, but it was kind of boring to ride by myself. I thought about reading one of my summer reading book, but decided to save those for rainy days. An hour had passed and I was still tossing the ball and mulling over my options.

"I win," Timmy said as he burst through the door. "Man, you had no idea where I was, did you?"

Wow, I totally forgot to even look for him. I couldn't believe he stayed in his spot for almost an hour. That's awesome, I thought.

"Yeah, you got me," I said, playing along. "I looked everywhere."

"I knew it," he said. "I knew you'd never find me."

And with that, he ran down the hall, very pleased that he had beat me at hide and seek. Still unsure of what to do with my free day, I ended up at the computer downstairs. While I hadn't planned on doing any research, I was kind of bored and decided to check out our next stop until I thought of something. The next trip would be our last Jersey Shore trip for a while, so I looked up Monmouth Beach. It took a while to find it because I spelled it twelve different ways, none of which were the right way. When I finally found some websites, I was excited again. No matter how tired I was, seeing a new place to explore was always exciting. I stumbled upon Monmouth's history and took some notes. I knew T-Bone would want to know all about it.

Nestled between the Atlantic Ocean and Shrewsbury River, Monmouth Beach has a history that dates way back to 1668, when the land, including Sea Bright, was purchased by Eliakim Wardell. In 1842, the property was in the hands of Wardell's great-grandson, Henry, who sold one of the lots to the U.S. Life-Saving Service, and the rest, in 1865, to Arthur V. Conover of Freehold. Mr. Conover purchased the land from Wardell for just $5.00 an acre, and soon after sold lots for $100.00 an acre.

Wow, $5.00 an acre! I wished I could buy a beach town for $5.00 an acre. I was pretty broke, though, so it would have to be a small town. I googled some pictures and decided it would be a great place to check out. It wasn't a Wildwood or Seaside type of resort, but it looked really nice. Since I didn't think there would be a lot to do, I decided to keep looking up more towns. Following Ocean Avenue north would bring us to Sea Bright and after that Sandy Hook. I knew there were more light-houses and I also knew if we continued driving along the edge of New Jersey, there was an amusement park in Keansburg.

I took some notes and then grabbed my glove. While I tossed the ball, I couldn't believe how boring it was without T-Bone. I was so bored; I found Timmy and asked him to have a catch.

"Nope," he said.

"What?" I asked, in complete shock. "Did you say no?"

"Yup," he said.

"Yup, you said nope, or yup you want to have a catch?" I tried to clarify.

"Yup, I don't want to play catch," he explained and walked away.

That was the first time he had ever turned me down. For anything. Ever. Maybe he figured out that I never looked for him during hide and seek.

Later that day, T-Bone stopped by and we decided to head to Monmouth Beach the next morning. Surprisingly, my grandfather volunteered. I thought for sure that our last trip wiped him out, but I was wrong.

The next morning, I woke up early and went downstairs to get my things together. My dad was sitting at the kitchen table and when I said, "Good morning," he didn't answer. Before I could say it again the phone rang. I tried to pretend I wasn't listening, but it seemed serious. "Uh-huh," my dad said several times. "I see, I see. Okay, I'll see you then. Thanks, goodbye."

Suddenly, my dad realized I was standing there.

"Hey, good morning," he said quietly. "Where are you boys off to?"

"Monmouth Beach to Keansburg," I answered. "Are you going to work?"

"Thankfully, I am," he said with a smile. I hadn't seen him grin in a long time and this looked like a genuine smile. "My company was bought, but the new owners want to keep everything the same for right now."

"Just for right now?" I asked, wondering why he didn't seem upset about that.

"Yeah," he smiled. "But, compared to so many other people, it could be worse."

I still didn't think it was great news, but I guess when you have four kids and you're afraid of losing your job, anything is better. I decided to be relieved, too.

My grandfather picked me up and then we got T-Bone and his usual gear. Looking back, we probably should have just kept his umbrella and chairs in my grandfather's trunk for the whole summer.

Our first stop was Monmouth Beach and it reminded me of many of the northern shore towns we had visited. There wasn't a boardwalk filled with rides and games; instead, there were huge Victorian homes and big mansions. We parked near the water and looked out at the waves. With the sun shining, the sounds of crashing waves and seagulls, and the smell of the salt air, it was a perfect day.

We watched a family playing volleyball on the beach and wondered if they actually knew the object of the game. Their serves rarely cleared the net and if the ball somehow managed to reach the other side, it usually landed in the sand. If I hadn't seen their faces, I would have guessed they were blindfolded. Despite being unable to serve or return the ball, they were having a great time. We also spotted a little boy attempting to build a sand castle. We watched him run to the water and lay his bucket sideways to fill it up. Unfortunately, each time he ran back to his mother the bucket was empty. He kind of reminded me of T-Bone.

We headed to the car and drove north to our next stop, Sea Bright, the southern end of the Sandy Hook peninsula. Sea Bright also held the distinction of being the easternmost point on New Jersey. I read that the first hotel opened in 1842 and offered excellent fishing, fine sea bathing and capital accommodations for 300 people.

There were several private beach clubs, so the public beach wasn't overcrowded. The town had several shops and restaurants and I knew my mom could definitely do some damage if she had come along, especially if my dad wasn't with us.

We continued our journey north to Sandy Hook, a 1,665-acre barrier peninsula with a view of the Manhattan skyline, discovered in the 1600s by explorer Henry Hudson. I knew T-Bone would love the history and the lighthouses.

"You know," said my grandfather, "if you visit Sandy Hook on a weekend, you have to leave early. They get so busy, they close the gates when they run out of parking."

"How can a town close the gates?" asked T-Bone.

"Sandy Hook isn't a town," my grandfather explained. "It's owned by the federal government. Most of it is managed by the National Parks as the Sandy Hook Unit of Gateway National Recreation Area."

"Good thing it's not a town," T-Bone laughed. "That would be some address."

"So do they have beaches or just trails?" I asked, growing more anxious to get there.

"Some of the finest beaches around," said my grandfather. "On the eastern shore you have three public beaches: North Beach, Gunnison Beach, and South Beach. The southern section has public beaches, fishing areas, and the Sea Gull's Nest, a seafood restaurant."

"That's cool," I said, "having so many beaches on one island."

"Actually, it's a peninsula because it's attached," my grandfather explained. "Although until they built a sea wall, there were times when the water flowed over the most narrow section and it became an island."

"Wow," T-Bone gasped. "Imagine spending the day on the beach and finding out you're stuck on an island?"

"Is Gunnison Beach the fort?" I asked.

"No, that's one of the largest clothing optional beaches on the East Coast," my grandfather laughed. "The fort you're referring to is Fort Hancock."

"Wait a minute," said T-Bone, holding up his hand. "Did you just say clothing-optional?"

"That's what I said," my grandfather nodded.

"Well, I don't get it," T-Bone wondered aloud, "what else can you wear if you don't wear clothing? A barrel? A suit of armor? That doesn't make any sense. If clothing is optional that means people don't have to wear any and that wouldn't make any sense."

My grandfather and I laughed when we realized T-Bone didn't know it was a naturalist beach. When we told him on that particular beach you can wear clothes or not wear clothes, he turned bright red. Then he quickly changed the subject.

"Is the fort still there?" asked T-Bone.

"It sure is," said my grandfather. "They only closed it in 1974. Its purpose was to protect the New York Harbor."

"How could a New Jersey fort protect New York?" I wondered.

"You know, you can see the New York City skyline from Sandy Hook," my grandfather explained. "We're very close. In fact, this is a very popular beach for New Yorkers, as it's only a short ferry ride to get here."

"It must be expensive," I added, remembering how expensive things were when my family went to New York City.

"Actually, you just pay to park," said my grandfather. "Your father would love this place."

We drove up Route 36, the only road onto the peninsula. My grandfather explained that Sandy Hook was still growing as a result of waves pushing sand from the southern end to the northern end.

We decided to drive up to Fort Hancock and the lighthouse and swim after lunch. The fort was amazing and right up T-Bone's alley. Thankfully, someone in the Army was smart enough to make sure everything was decommissioned before T-Bone arrived. We read that before it was the famous Aberdeen Proving Grounds in Maryland, it was actually the Sandy Hook Proving Grounds.

When we finished touring the fort, we headed to the lighthouse. It resembled Abby and Barney, the tower-style lighthouses in Absecon and Barnegat, and had the honor of being the oldest operating lighthouse in the country. When T-Bone realized it was still being lit, he was anxious to meet the old keeper. I think he thought a man would appear, looking just like the men in the black-and-white pictures we saw at each lighthouse. While he was a little disappointed that there was no old keeper, he was happy the Coast Guard maintained the light.

"Hey, listen to this," T-Bone began. "This lighthouse was originally called the New York Lighthouse and it was built while we were still colonies and they paid for it with a lottery."

"Like the Jersey Cash 5?" I asked.

"Let's just say similar," my grandfather laughed. "You know, this lighthouse was once 500 feet from the tip; now it's over a mile and a half away."

"They moved an old lighthouse?" asked T-Bone.

"No," I said, shaking my head, "remember my grandfather said that the peninsula was growing because the water moved the sand to the north?"

"Oh, that's right," T-Bone remembered.

"Here's an interesting fact," I said while reading, "during the Revolution, the British had control of the lighthouse for most of the war and it's so strong that an hour of cannon fire didn't put a dent in it."

"No wonder it still works," said T-Bone. "My dad always says they don't make things like they used to."

We checked out the site and realized we were getting hungry. We headed to Parking Lot D, as my grandfather knew about a restaurant called the Sea Gulls' Nest. Twenty-five feet above ground, with three decks, it offered amazing views of the Sandy Hook Bay and the Atlantic Ocean. We decided on burgers since we would need our energy for the beach. Our waitress reminded us to check out the Twin Lights of Navesink, another famous lighthouse that was very close.

When we finished eating we headed to, as T-Bone called it, a clothing-mandatory beach. There were plenty of people, but it wasn't wall-to-wall umbrellas. We left our boogie boards in the car and decided to just swim. My grandfather sat under the umbrella and seemed to enjoy the warm breeze and the people-watching. Luckily, everyone here had a bathing suit.

After a couple of hours we decided to move on. Even though we could have happily stayed all day, we had another lighthouse and a couple more towns to visit. We drove west to Highlands, which was right outside the park. This was one of the places where people who visit Sandy Hook like to stay. There were shops, restaurants, inns and hotels, as well as amazing views. We went directly to the Twin Lights of Navesink Lighthouse. It was the first time we saw two lighthouses together like that. It was one building with a lighthouse on each side. It was used as the primary lighthouse for New York Harbor and was known as the best and the brightest light in North America.

We entered the enormous building and it was very impressive. Even though the lights were no longer lit, it was interesting to stand in a place that was built in 1828 and was so important in its day. Having two lighthouses, we wondered how the keeper was able to manage. We read that there was one primary keeper and three assistants. Their main duty was to maintain the light from sunset to sunrise. Other duties included trimming the wick, winding the clockwork mechanism that rotated the light, replenishing the oil supply, and later when the South Tower was electrified, ensuring the machinery in the powerhouse was operating all night long. The keepers also had to maintain the buildings and grounds.

It was a difficult job and the assistants requested they be allowed to work in shifts through the night as a result of the cold, damp conditions. It was so perilous that one keeper accidentally lit himself on fire and lighthouse keepers received little formal training. Most of them learned their duties on the job. Many were former sea captains, sailors or military men who were appointed to their positions by the federal government. Yearly salaries were based on experience and rank, and ranged from $400-$600 in 1861, to a top salary of $1000 in 1921.

"I always thought this would have been a really fun job, lighting the house every night, waving to the boats, and never having to commute," said T-Bone. "I thought they just lit the light at sunset and turned it off at sunrise."

"I have to admit," I said, "I thought there was more than turning a light on and off, but I didn't think it was this hard."

"Hey, if we lived near here back then, they might have hired us to cut the grass for them," he smiled.

"On $600 per year?" I laughed. "I doubt it."

When we left the lighthouse we drove along the coast, checking out the boat marina. Shrewsbury Avenue was the closest to the water and gave us great views. The restaurants had cool nautical names like Bahr's Landing, Wind and Sea, the Inlet Café, and the Clam Hut. We drove over to Bay Avenue and Shore Drive. As we

145

continued, we found ourselves in Atlantic Highlands, the highest point on the eastern seaboard, south of Maine.

"What about High Point?" T-Bone said, referring to our trip to High Point State Park.

"That's the highest point in the whole state," I said. "This is the highest point along the coast for the entire eastern seaboard, south of Maine."

"What?" he asked, very confused.

"Let me," said my grandfather. "Along the coast, the elevation is usually low, so they're not the highest for the whole state because when you go inland we have mountains. But for the eastern states that border the ocean, this is the highest coastal point, south of Maine."

"Okay," he said, although we weren't sure he really got it.

"In fact," said my grandfather, "this is where the Lenape Indians first encountered Europeans, and soon were trading with them. Fifty-six years after Henry Hudson's 1609 visit, English settlers bought the whole peninsula from the Lenape and called it Portland Poynt."

"How do you know that?" I asked, very impressed that my grandfather knew these amazing details.

"I read some of your brochures when you boys were in the ocean," he smiled. "The municipal harbor is the largest on the east coast and since 1986 they have had high-speed ferry service to New York City. They have eight town-owned parks, two county parks, the nine-mile Henry Hudson Trail, a maritime museum and the Strauss Mansion Museum that you can check out next time."

"Wow, how long were we in the ocean?" T-Bone asked, amazed my grandfather remembered so much.

We drove along Route 36 through small towns like Leonardo, Belford, and Port Monmouth. We saw a sign for Bayshore Waterfront Park in Port Monmouth and decided to check it out. The 227-acre park had a fishing pier and amazing views. It was also the home of the Bayshore Waterfront Park Activity Center, which was now the Seabrook-Wilson House, one of the oldest surviving houses in the region. The large frame building, dating back to the early 1700s, was constructed in several phases over the course of two hundred years.

"That owner must have had some patience," said T-Bone. "If I was building a house and it took 200 years, I would demand my money back or at least make them throw in a free swing set or pool."

"How would you know if it took 200 years?" I asked. "Do you plan on living to be 200 years old?"

"Good point," he agreed. "If it took 100 years, I would definitely ask for my money back."

"No, no, no," my grandfather said, shaking his head, "they kept adding to it and it took over 200 years to get to this point."

We headed north again, through North Middletown to Keansburg. This was going to be good. Keansburg was the home of the Keansburg Amusement Park and Runaway Rapids Water Park.

"Can we go in the water park and the amusement park?" asked T-Bone.

"How else can you write about it?" asked my grandfather. It was a Buy One, Get One Free day and we could go in the water park and then do the amusement park. We parked in a lot and looked for the main entrance.

"Excuse me," T-Bone said as he approached a woman with a bulky double stroller loaded with bags and kids, "how do you get in?"

"Excuse me?" she replied while wrestling a lollipop out of the little boy's hand. "In where?"

"Inside the amusement park," he said as if she had three heads.

"You *are* inside the amusement park," she replied, as if he had four heads.

"Hey, this is like a permanent carnival with much better

rides," I noticed. "Look, you don't have to pay to walk in, you just buy tickets or a bracelet and come and go as you please."

"I don't get it," said T-Bone, "what if you don't buy a ticket? You're still allowed to walk around?"

"Sure, why not?" I laughed. I really liked the idea of meandering around. This amusement park was different than some of the other ones I had been to. It wasn't fancy; it was old-school in a good way, with rides for everyone, games, and a ton of food stands. It reminded me of some big amusement parks that try to copy this atmosphere, except this was authentic. And maybe they were able to keep the prices low because they didn't fence people out.

"Look," said T-Bone, pointing to his watch, "we need to get to the water park so we have enough time."

The water park was definitely newer than the amusement park and we hit every single ride, from the Mountain Blast to the Power Tower to the Crazy Lazy River. It was a great setup; big enough, but not too big. And my grandfather found a nice place to relax in the shade. By 5:30, we were wiped out. We decided to dry off and get something to eat. The only problem would be deciding what to eat. The stands had so many different food choices. We opted for pizza and lemonade and then strategically planned each ride we would go on.

We decided to start with the roller coaster and end with the go-karts. Since our bracelets were for unlimited rides, we were definitely going to get our money's worth. I was still surprised at how well my grandfather kept up with us, although he always found a bench once we were in line. When we finished the rides we checked out the fishing pier. It was 2,500 feet long and right behind the amusement park.

"Hey, check out the ocean," said T-Bone.

"That's not the ocean," I said. "We left the ocean when we left Sandy Hook."

"You're wrong, Nick," he said with a know-it-all smile. "See this water? This is the Atlantic Ocean."

"No, T, you're wrong," I laughed. "Ask anybody here. I dare you."

"Well, I won't ask your grandfather; naturally he'd be on your side," he said as he analyzed all of the people on the pier. He walked up to an older man and asked him if he knew the name of the water.

"Whaddya think, I'm a moron?" the man said and turned his back.

"Excuse me, Miss," he said to a woman who was walking by with a small boy. "Do you know the name of this water?"

"What?" she asked.

"The name of this water," T-Bone repeated. "Do you know it? My friend is saying that this is not the ocean."

"It's not the Atlantic Ocean," the little boy said and laughed. "It's the Raritan Bay. You lose. Mommy, that big boy loses."

"Are you sure?" T-Bone kneeled down and asked.

"I'm five years old," the little boy said, holding up five fingers. "I even knowed that wasn't the ocean when I was four years old."

"Hmmm," T-Bone processed the information, "you even knowed it when you were four, huh?"

"So?" I asked, waiting for my formal, public apology.

"So, let's walk on the pier that is over the *Raritan Bay*," he said.

Once again, it was hard to believe that we did so many things in one day. I decided that when we wrote our reports, we should remind families that we see so much in one day because we see it and move on. I wanted to make sure families knew they could spend an entire day at Sandy Hook, or Keansburg, or Asbury Park, or Atlantic City. In fact, they could spend several days and never be bored. My grandfather always said that the key was

151

realistic planning. If we had my sisters with us, we probably would have been home after the water park.

On the way home, my grandfather decided to drive a little more north through some more harbor and bay towns. We drove through Union Beach, Keyport Harbor, Cliffwood Beach, Laurence Harbor, and finished at the Raritan Bay Waterfront Park in South Amboy. It was just about dark and we could see the playground, huge gazebo, and an incredible view of New York City. We all bowed our heads as we approached the Victims of Terrorism Memorial and then headed back to the car.

"So, boys, what do you think?" my grandfather asked.

"I think I want to come back and spend one day at Sandy Hook and one day at Keansburg," T-Bone nodded.

"Me too," I agreed and then sarcastically asked, "but who could we ever find to take us?"

"Are you kidding?" said T-Bone. "When people read these reports, they'll be lined up to take us."

"I was thinking my grandfather," I laughed.

"Do you think he'd want to come back?" T-Bone whispered.

"Try and stop him," my grandfather whispered over T-Bone's shoulder and laughed.

Chapter Eleven
The Great Debate

It actually took us a whole week to work on our videos and write our reports. We decided to write separate reports; one for Sandy Hook, the Twin Lights and Highlands and the other for Atlantic Highlands to South Amboy. We really wanted kids and their families to have enough time to enjoy everything and figured this would help them plan fun trips.

As I uploaded the last video, T-Bone came walking in my room.

"Are you ready for the big day?" he asked.

"If you mean Tuesday being slightly better than Monday but not nearly as good as a weekend, then yes," I said, having no idea what he was referring to.

"You forgot about today?" he asked with astonishment.

I stared at him for a few moments, trying to find a clue. His clothes weren't helping me, his shoes weren't helping me, and he had nothing in his hands. I tried to think very hard before I let him tell me what I had apparently forgotten. It was no use. I had nothing.

"Uh, our big debate is today," he said with his arms outstretched.

"What?" I asked. "I don't remember a big debate. I don't remember having a first debate, just practices."

"Yeah, the first one was cancelled. I forgot to tell you."

"I signed us up for this one on the day my mom and I went shopping," he explained as if I should have known that. "I'm pretty sure I told you."

"I'm pretty sure you didn't," I defended myself.

"Well, that's neither here nor there," he said. "Let's go."

"Wait a minute," I said. "What's with the *here nor there?* And who is debating?"

"I don't know about the *here nor there,* I heard it on television and thought it sounded smart, no?" he said, trying to see if his new expression sounded smart.

"No," I flatly answered.

"And we, you and I, are debating each other at the library, at 1:00, in front of everyone."

"Whoa, whoa," I said, vigorously shaking my head. "I'm not debating anyone at 1:00 today. There's a Phillies day game and I'll be downstairs with a bag of chips and a lemonade. Good luck, though."

"Don't be ridiculous, you have to come," he insisted. "I can't debate myself."

"Actually," I pretended to mull his last statement over, "I think you could."

"Very funny," he laughed. "Now come on, let's go."

As much as I hated to speak in front of people, and as much as I hated to debate, I kind of felt sorry for T-Bone. He was so excited about this debate and if I didn't go, he couldn't go. He was still staring at me with that goofy smile and I knew there was no way for me to get out of this without crushing him. This must have been how parents felt when their kids begged them to squeeze into those goofy kiddie rides at amusement parks over and over again.

"What's the topic?" I asked.

"That's beauty of it," he said. "We get to pick the topic,

so here's my plan. I'll take the Northern Jersey Shores and you take the Southern Jersey Shores and we'll debate which is better. And it won't matter who wins because, either way, New Jersey will be the winner."

"That doesn't even seem like a real topic," I protested.

"Come on, you've got younger brothers and sisters," he pointed out, "and you know anything can be debated. What to watch on television, whose turn it is to bat, what to share for a snack. Right?"

"I guess," I said, feeling like he was winning the debate over what a debate topic could be.

"Okay, are we good?" he asked, heading to the door. "Are we ready?"

"No," I said, "not even close. I'm not prepared."

"There's no studying for this topic," he insisted, "this is all about our day trips and how you feel."

We arrived at the library, parked our bikes, and walked in. I was hoping there wouldn't be anyone to watch, but there were twenty chairs set up and people walking around. T-Bone went up to speak with Miss Albert and before I knew it, people were seated and I was standing at a podium.

"I'd like to welcome everyone to the First Annual Library

Debate," she began. "I'd like to introduce our two debaters, Nicky and Tommy."

At that point, camera flashes started going off. Interestingly, it seemed like all of the people were taking pictures of Miss Albert. She introduced our topic and T-Bone got to go first.

"I'd like to thank all of you for being here for this very important New Jersey debate," T-Bone began. "Today, in our debate to determine which are the best Jersey Shores, the northern portion or the southern portion, I will support the theory that while they are all worthy shores, the Northern Shores have much more to offer."

Wow, I thought, he totally prepared for this. If I wasn't standing there I would have thought he was reading off of a teleprompter. I could feel my tongue start to swell even though I knew it was all in my head. Suddenly, I noticed Miss Albert point at me, while she posed for a picture.

"Well, I, uh, I would, uh, like to thank all of you, for coming, too," I stumbled, "even though I have no idea who any of you are."

As soon as I said that, the audience laughed and I could feel my nervousness slip away, *a little*. I started wishing I knew more jokes.

"I agree with my opponent that the entire shore is, uh, you know, great, and I will discuss the, you know, good things about the Southern Shore," I continued, very aware that I needed to stop saying the words *you know* and *uh*.

"I'd like to start with history," T-Bone declared. "Take Keansburg on the Raritan Bay. This amusement park is New Jersey's oldest and provides families with a day of old-fashioned fun. The carousel house is from an 1899 expo in Philadelphia and William Gelhaus paid to have it dismantled and brought over by horse and wagon. Stepping into the Keansburg Amusement Park is an affordable way to step back in time."

Wow, I thought, when did he read that? I needed something to match it, so I went with Historic Cold Spring Village. Now, I just had to speak without tripping over my colossal tongue.

"I agree, Keansburg is very much like a time machine and really fun, but for history at the Jersey Shore, I recommend Historic Cold Spring Village in beautiful Cape May," I began. "The whole village was assembled one building at a time and it's a living history museum where you can meet with, and actually speak to, costumed re-enactors. It's a chance to really experience early American life."

That wasn't too bad, I thought. I decided that instead of trying to plan out each sentence as I was speaking, I would pretend my mind was like a file cabinet. When I decided on a topic, I would pretend to open the file cabinet and pull out the file on that particular place to remind me what I loved. Since I loved all of the places we visited, I didn't even have to make anything up. I just hoped that I could continue to remember important facts.

"Next, I'd like to discuss lighthouses," said T-Bone. "The oldest operating lighthouse is in Sandy Hook, which is located at Fort Hancock. A visit to this lighthouse is like getting two great pieces of history for the very reasonable price of one. And, located right outside the park is the Twin Lights of Navesink, which played an important role in assisting ships through the very important New York Harbor. In addition, one of my personal favorites is the Sea Girt Lighthouse."

"This is true," I agreed, "but I would also include the Absecon, the Barnegat, Hereford, and the Cape May lighthouses. Amazing lighthouses have played a critical role in New Jersey's history and Old Barney was even a lookout in WWI. They each have wonderful stories of their history and how they helped the state and towns."

So far, I was keeping up, but I'd have to keep those files coming quick. I had a feeling T-Bone memorized a script.

"My next point will be family fun, and the obvious choice would be Point Pleasant with its amazing beaches, boardwalks, piers, and even an aquarium," he said. "It's a place to relax and make memories."

Okay, he's really stepping up his game, I thought. So I quickly went through the old mental files.

"Family fun is important," I agreed, "and I would send families to the wonderful boardwalk at Ocean City. This town was born for family fun and provides a great atmosphere for families to spend time together."

He wanted to go with making memories and I pulled out the word atmosphere without stumbling. I wished there was a scoreboard so I could see how I was doing. I knew he was probably winning, but I had to be close.

"Well, for more family fun, I would suggest Seaside, the *real* Seaside," he suggested. "It's an example of what makes the *real* Jersey Shore so unique. There is a carousel at the Casino Pier which was saved from a fire at the Burlington Island Amusement Park. And I highly recommend the games of chance."

"Seaside is wonderful, but let's not forget Wildwood with its wide, free beaches, boardwalk attractions, piers and water parks," I reminded him. "Wildwood has been hosting families for many, many years and is legendary."

"If you're looking for legendary relaxation, I would recommend Long Branch," said T-Bone. "Seven U.S. presidents couldn't have been wrong, and the Pier Village makes spending the day convenient and exciting. Plus, you can follow up a traditional Jersey Burger at *Stewarts* with amazing desserts at *Cake, Bake, and Roll.*"

Really? He was bringing U.S. presidents and food into the debate. Okay, I needed to think. I wished I could

160

snap my fingers and freeze time, gather my thoughts, and unfreeze time. Since I didn't have time to challenge the laws of physics, I went with Long Beach Island.

"Relaxation is a wonderful thing," I began, "and LBI has something for everyone, from quiet beaches to Bay Village shops as well as a peaceful bay. And if you're looking for something for the kids, there's always Fantasy Island, Thundering Surf Water Park, Bill Burr's Flamingo Golf and Big Dipper for amazing ice cream."

"That reminds me of one of my favorite spots; Asbury Park, filled with history, culture, and a strong tradition of music," remembered T-Bone. "You can walk the boards, play mini-golf while you learn about the town's many contributions to music, and cool off on a boardwalk water playground. And, of course, there's always the ocean."

Well done, I thought. That was a good one, but I had one last trick up my sleeve.

"Asbury Park does have a wonderful boardwalk," I agreed, "which reminds me of Atlantic City, the first boardwalk in the world at a lengthy six miles. In addition to the casinos, there's Ripley's Believe It or Not, an aquarium, a fountain show inside the Pier Shops, and the Absecon Lighthouse is just down the road. And, of course, there's always the ocean."

I hoped he was done because my brain was starting to hurt. It was both exciting and awesome to go head-to-head and I was up against a pro. I felt like I held my own and I hoped I did the shore towns of South Jersey justice. Now, I just needed to think of a conclusion while T-Bone rattled off what was sure to be a long, long ending.

"In conclusion," he started, "the entire Jersey Shore is unique. Whether you go north or south, you are sure to have a great time and if we did our jobs debating, the real winners will be the people who take our advice and visit these great resorts and towns. Thank you."

Oh, no, I thought. Not only was that much quicker than I thought it would be, it was really good. What could I possibly say that could compete with that? At this point, I couldn't try to push people to my side because he already declared the audience the winners. I couldn't declare the audience the winners, which was a brilliant idea, because he had already done so. As people clapped for him, I started telling myself to think, think, think. When the applause died down, I took a deep breath.

"Ditto," I said.

The room remained quiet. The audience couldn't tell if I was joking or if that was really my conclusion, so they stared at me. Ten seconds seemed like ten hours of loud silence. I could feel my face turning red and then, just like the friend I knew he was, T-Bone started clapping. Suddenly, everyone was clapping and my answer didn't sound so bad. It was almost as if T-Bone's clapping gave them permission to like it, like a seal of approval.

162

Miss Albert came up to the podiums and had tears in her eyes. Her family started taking her picture again and I think we may have gotten in one this time. When the room quieted down, Miss Albert started to speak. "When I decided to start a debate club, I wasn't sure if any children would be interested," she began. "Then I met Nicky and Tommy. Tommy was eager to debate and Nick mentioned something about public speaking making his tongue swell."

Everyone started to smile and laugh.

"But I have to say," she continued, "that this was one of the best debates I have ever witnessed. Their positions were well-supported, clearly stated, and lively. These boys have debated better than many adults and I couldn't be prouder. Please, let's give them another round of applause."

As the audience clapped, I felt pretty good. For T-Bone, this was just another day at the office, but for me, it was like conquering a major fear. I actually stood in front of a room full of people and, with absolutely no preparation, debated a pretty good talker. And T-Bone was right, we may have motivated someone to go visit a New Jersey Shore. As we headed to the refreshment table, T-Bone was pumped and grinning ear to ear.

"Wasn't that awesome?" he gushed. "That was such a rush. Did you see everyone clapping for us and smiling? This was great. By the way, nice job."

"That was pretty cool," I admitted. "I think *you* were born to speak in public."

"Don't sell yourself short," he laughed. "You kept right up with me…well, until you said *ditto*!"

"Yeah, thanks for the save," I said, knowing that it was T-Bone who saved my nervous, one-word conclusion. It was at that point that I realized debating was T-Bone's sport. Some kids have soccer or baseball, but the thing that made T-Bone feel alive was talking. He liked to play sports, but I couldn't recall ever seeing him this happy about any sport.

When I got home, I walked in with a trophy that had a man on the top with his arm extended and his mouth open. It looked like he was singing opera, although I didn't think they gave opera singers trophies. It was actually the oddest trophy I had ever seen and on the name plate it said "Great Debater".

"Wow, what's that?" asked my mom.

"I won a trophy for debating T-Bone," I said.

"Did you have to sing?" asked Timmy.

"No, I think he's supposed to be speaking," I explained.

"I think you're wrong," said Timmy. "The guy on that trophy is definitely singing."

"Let me see," my mom said as she ran over to see it. "Look at that, "Great Debater" trophy. I'm so proud of you for trying something new. Why didn't you tell us you had a debate? We would have come."

"I didn't even know myself," I shrugged. "T-Bone told me about it five minutes before it started."

"And you still beat him?" asked Timmy.

"No," I laughed. "I don't think anyone can beat T-Bone at talking."

"But you got the "Great Debater" trophy," he insisted, "so you must have won."

"I know," I told him, "but T-Bone got the "Greater Debater" trophy."

"Oh," Timmy said. "That's okay, second place is still good. How many guys did you compete against?"

"Just T-Bone," I laughed.

"Oh," he said. "Well, it's the thought that counts."

My mom and I laughed. Timmy didn't realize what a victory this was for me. I was happy for T-Bone. He deserved that trophy; in fact, he even deserved a trophy with a better guy on it. But for me, the trophy wasn't the big deal. I had a lot of nice trophies and ribbons. This was different. This is what it must feel like when people do something like climb a mountain or learn to cliff-dive. My mom said that sort of victory should be celebrated. While she loaded my sisters in the van, Timmy and T-Bone were still admiring the trophy. I couldn't believe I debated someone, especially T-Bone.

"Where are we going?" I asked.

"For some hot dogs at Captain Paul's," she smiled.

"Cool," said T-Bone, "we're going to the shore."

"What?" I asked.

"Your mom said we're going to see Captain Paul," he said, rolling his eyes. "Clearly he's a boat captain, right, Mrs. A.?"

"It's Captain Paul's Firehouse Dogs," she laughed.

"So we're not going to the shore?" asked T-Bone.

"No, Captain Paul's Firehouse Dogs is in Lawrenceville," she explained. "It's one of my favorite places."

"So is Captain Paul a *retired* fisherman?" asked T-Bone, missing the obvious explanation.

"No, he's the captain of a soccer team," I sarcastically replied.

"Seriously?" asked T-Bone.

"No," I laughed. "He's obviously a fire department captain. You know, *Firehouse Dogs*, get it?"

"Oh, that's pretty clever," he said. "Now I get it. That's pretty funny."

When we arrived, we walked inside and there were several stools at the counter. It wasn't huge, but there were plenty of tables outside, also.

"Hey, how are you guys doing?" said a friendly man from behind the counter. "Can you believe what a beautiful day it is?"

"Couldn't ask for a nicer one," said my mom.

"That's for sure," he smiled. "And look at this good-looking crowd you brought in."

"There's five of us," said Maggie as she pointed to each kid and counted. "If you add my mom, then it's five kids plus one mom."

"Smart and cute," he smiled. "So what are you guys in the mood for today?"

"Hop dawgs," yelled Emma from beneath her pink sunglasses. "And fwench fwies, too."

"Well, you're at the right place," he said as he grabbed a pad to write the orders and looked at my mom. "How do they want the dogs?"

While my mom ordered, T-Bone looked surprised.

"Is that guy like your uncle?" he asked.

"Like my uncle?" I said. "This is the first time I ever met him."

"You think he's that nice to everybody?"

Before I could answer, two paramedics and two police officers walked in.

"Hey, here's the calvary. Come on in, guys. I'll be right with you," smiled the man behind the counter, proving that he was, indeed, that nice to everybody.

While my mom ordered for the girls, Timmy, T-Bone and I looked over the menu. Every item included firefighting, police, ambulance and medical words. There was the Trooper, a fried hot dog with potatoes, peppers and mustard; the First Alarm, a hot dog with cheese; and the Chief, a hot dog topped with Italian chili. There were many different hot dogs, sausage, meatballs, fries, nachos, onion rings, and even ice cream.

My mom suggested we all try the Trooper. She said when she was a kid her dad would take her family to a famous place that used to be in Trenton called the Casino for a Casino Dog.

"They let kids in a casino?" asked T-Bone in disbelief. "Were you born in the Wild West?"

"It wasn't a real casino," she said. "It was a Trenton landmark; everyone went there, and the most popular item was the Casino Dog with potatoes and peppers."

"You had me at hot dog," I said.

"Me too," said T-Bone and Timmy.

We placed our orders and found out that the nice man behind the counter was actually Captain Paul, a real retired fire captain from Trenton. We told him all of our names and about how my dad stopped in the Calhoun Street firehouse when we first started our Garden State adventures. He was so nice that we felt like we had known him forever.

"Listen," he said, "why don't you bring the kids outside and I'll have Katie or Angel bring the food out."

"Thanks so much," my mom smiled and ushered everyone to a table under a big umbrella.

Captain Paul's was really cool. There was fire memorabilia everywhere and the wall was covered with patches from departments all over the country.

After a few minutes, Katie and Angel brought out our order and it was as good as my mom said it would be. After our hot dogs, we all had gelati, which was soft ice cream; then Italian ice, then more soft ice cream. It was brilliant, I thought. T-Bone was the only one who didn't have a gelati. He was so amazed to see a chocolate-dipped frozen banana on the menu, he couldn't resist. Before we left, we said goodbye to our new freind Captain Paul and promised we'd be back.

On the way home, my mom asked me all about our debate and when I got to my brilliant conclusion, she laughed so hard she almost cried.

"*Ditto*?" she laughed. "You actually concluded with *ditto*? That's hysterical."

"I couldn't think of anything else," I admitted. "And I agreed with him, so ditto came out. You should have seen how quiet the room got."

When I told her how T-Bone saved the day, she wasn't at all surprised.

"Debating is exhausting," I said. "As soon as we get home, I'm going to bed. I'm beat."

"Ditto," she laughed.

Chapter Twelve
Onward and Upward

The next morning we put the last of our reports on a memory stick and my mom drove us to the State House. We took our jobs seriously and I hoped Billy would like our work. When we arrived he was standing in the hallway and came right up to us.

"Hey, boys," he said, "your reports have gone over really well. I'm sending copies to the legislators so they can see what a great job you are doing."

"That reminds me," I said, "have they voted on us yet?"

"Not yet," he smiled. "We all wish things moved faster around here, but it does take time. I'll let you know as soon as I hear something."

I kind of hoped when we walked in that he would have told us it was official that *we* were official. That's okay, I thought, I'm sure the Assembly and Senate are pretty busy.

"Can you come into my office?" Billy asked.

"Sure," my mom answered for us.

We sat in the big leather chairs and felt very important as we looked around his office. His desk was kind of messy but his office was very neat. He had lots of pictures hanging on the wall and all over his desk. In most of the pictures he was shaking someone's hand, but there was one picture on his desk of a little boy.

"Is that your son?" asked T-Bone.

"No," Billy said softly, "that's a very special little boy. His name was Joey Angiolino."

"Was?" I asked, hoping I had heard him wrong.

"Very, very sadly, yes," he explained. "Joey died from a disease called Hurler's Syndrome. He was only 15 months old, but he was a very special little guy."

"Wow," I said, totally not expecting him to say that. "I'm really sorry."

"Me too," he said. "The community really rallied for

him, but by July he had fought as hard as he could."

"That's just awful," my mom said, gazing at his little smile. "I've never heard of Hurler's Syndrome. Is it rare?"

"Unfortunately, yes," said Billy. "He was being treated at Duke University Medical Center in North Carolina, but rare diseases get so little attention and even less funding."

"That reminds me of our friend, Ryan Schultz," said T-Bone. "He's a strong kid and we've donated money to help find a cure for him. His mom is a teacher in Hamilton."

"Ironically," said Billy, "little Joey's mother, father and grandmother are also teachers in Hamilton. In fact, Joey's grandmother teaches at the same schools as little Ryan's mom, Maria."

"Really?" I asked, suddenly understanding what people mean when they say small world.

"I wish we could have done something for him," said T-Bone.

"It's not too late," said Billy. "Go online and read about it and maybe you could write about him in one of your reports. So many families with kids follow your adventures. It might be a great way to get the word out and maybe raise money to find a cure."

"Do you think his parents would mind?" I asked, not sure if it would be the right thing to do.

"I think his parents, Nicole and James, would be touched, and I think that sharing his story could make other kids realize how lucky they are and motivate them to get involved," he replied. "The Duke Pediatric Blood and Marrow Transplant Family Support Program helped the family so much, maybe you could mention that, too."

"That's a great idea," my mother agreed. "Plus, I'm sure it would make Joey's parents proud to know he has touched so many people."

"Agreed," said Billy. "So if you want to do a special report about Joey, we'll put it on the website."

When we got in the car, we were still talking about little Ryan and Joey. We wondered how Ryan was doing and decided to grab some lunch at DeLorenzo's to check in with Sam. It was very busy, but he seemed really happy to see us. We told him all about the bills to make us *Official Junior Ambassadors* and he said he wasn't surprised.

"Have you seen Ryan Schultz and his family?" T-Bone asked.

"I sure have," he said. "They were in here last week and Ryan was doing well."

"That's good," I said. "Is his Ryan's Quest charity doing well, too?"

"They actually had a *Police Department versus Fire Department* hockey game to raise money for a cure," he said as he spun some dough. "It was a great event."

"Did they raise enough to cure it?" asked T-Bone.

"No," Sam smiled, "not enough for a cure, but every bit counts, and no one is giving up."

We finished our lunch, said goodbye to Sam, and made a decision. We agreed to take a week off from our day trips and spend the week doing odd jobs. We had so many customers patiently waiting for us and we could earn a lot of money. We decided that all of the money we earned would be divided between Ryan's Quest and the Duke PBMT Family Support Program. One charity helps Ryan and other little boys with Duchenne muscular dystrophy; the other would be in memory of Joey, and would help other kids who were very sick and their families.

On the way home, my mom drove through the town of Bordentown. It was nice with shops and restaurants and colonial houses on Farnsworth Avenue, the main street.

"Where are we going?" I asked.

"You'll see," my mom winked.

We pulled up to an old bank building, similar to the one in the City of Burlington, except it had a giant ice cream cone out front. The sign read *I Scream, U Scream*, and I had a good feeling about this stop.

"Your grandfather told me about this place," my mom explained. "It's amazing inside. Picture people coming in such a grand building to do their banking."

"This place is pretty cool," said T-Bone. "I wish my dad's bank served breakfast and lunch."

"We just ate tomato pie," I laughed. "We ought to focus on dessert. Plus, it's not a bank anymore."

And focus on dessert we did. We sat at a table and ate our sundaes while my mom remarked about what a fantastic building it was. We kept laughing at her, but inside, we both agreed. Being *Great Allies of History* and all, we could definitely appreciate eating ice cream in such an old bank. I decided we would have to come back and spend some time in Bordentown, especially at I Scream, U Scream.

When we got home, my mom grabbed the mail and there was a letter from Anne Salvatore at Historic Cold Spring Village. She thanked us for all of our work and enjoyed our Cape May report. She then invited us to speak at the Village's Spring Lecture series.

"Do we get to debate?" asked T-Bone.

"It says she would like us to speak to the group about how we're introducing New Jersey to New Jersey," I said as I read the letter.

"Can you really introduce something to itself?" asked T-Bone.

"I think she means you'll be introducing the state of New Jersey to the citizens of New Jersey who may not be aware of all the state has to offer," my mom suggested.

"That makes sense," I agreed. "But that would mean public speaking again."

"I know," T-Bone smiled. "Isn't it great?"

I had to admit that the thought of it made me a little nervous. Maybe the reason I did okay at the first debate was because I didn't have time to get nervous. It was practically a surprise. Now, I'd overthink this so much that I'd be a total flop.

"I don't know," I said. "I might want to stop while I'm ahead. You know, go out on a high note."

"No, no," T-Bone protested. "You're thinking about this all wrong. You're on a roll. You're a "Great Debater" now. You even have the trophy to prove it. We have to keep moving forward and never miss an opportunity to speak about New Jersey."

"I have a better idea," I suggested, trying to avoid giving a speech. "Let's use our pictures to make a PowerPoint presentation and we can narrate it in the dark."

"That's not bad," T-Bone said as he thought it over. "We could give our speeches and then show the pictures. That would really bring the state to life."

"No, no," I said, "I meant pictures *instead* of speeches."

"No, no," said T-Bone, "Pictures *and* speeches. Trust me. When we get done with this state, people will not only know where we are, they will know what we are all about. There will be a line around the state."

It was amazing. T-Bone never seemed to get rattled; never seemed to doubt himself if he thought he was doing something to help out. I couldn't figure out where he got the confidence. I wished I could always be that positive.

"What if," I began, "you do the speaking and I'll work the remote control for the slides."

T-Bone held up my trophy and pointed to my letter from the Governor. "Sorry, Nick, you're in," he smiled. "When it comes to speaking, I'm *pro* T-Bone *and* Nicky Fifth."

"Ditto," I laughed.

The End

Welcome to the
Franklin Mason Press
Guest Young Author Section

Turn this page for stories from our three newest Guest Young Authors, ages 9-12. From thousands of submissions, these stories were selected by a committee for their creativity, originality, and quality.

We believe that children should have an active role in literature, including publishing and sharing their stories with the world. We hope you will enjoy reading them as much as we did.

If you are 9-12 years old and would like to be a Franklin Mason Press Guest Young Author, read the directions, write your story, and send it in! The first, second, and third place winners receive $50.00, $40.00, and $30.00, respectively; a book, an award, and a party to autograph books. Send us a 150-350 word story about something strange, funny or unusual. Your story may be fiction or non-fiction. For additional details visit:

www.franklinmasonpress.com or
www.nickyfifth.com

1st Place Guest Young Author

Claire Ernst
Walter C. Black Elementary School
Hightstown, New Jersey

Stand Out

On the Sunday of Harvesting, Farmer Clank was out in the fields finding the best crops for his vegetable soup. His daughter and wife were around the corner sewing and stitching dresses for the fancy store on Mulberry Drive. Then, a flock of crows started flying down to the rows of carrots. Farmer Clank was on the other side of the farm so he didn't see it.

While the crows were grabbing crops, three of the nine birds that went there were laughing at one crow. That crow's name was Bob. I know that it's a silly name, but that's not why they were laughing. They were laughing at his one orange feather. He tried to fit in, but it was just impossible. He even tried to impress all of the other birds but it just didn't work. So when the farmer noticed this, he came up with a machine. That machine was an invention that could turn regular feathers into orange-colored   feathers. So he put all of the birds, except Bob, in the machine. Suddenly, they noticed that the feather wasn't that funny at all!

Soon, the birds and Bob became great friends and they found out that Bob was a very nice bird. They learned not to judge a bird by its feathers, and then they had some vegetable soup.

2nd Place Guest Young Author

Brielle Eike
Katharine D. Malone Elementary School
Rockaway, New Jersey

The Journey of the Lost Penguin

One chilly day, a little penguin named Pete was playing with his friends, Jesse, Alex, and Pablo. They went belly surfing on a very steep glacier near the North Pole. Pete went down first; he slid and slid until nobody could see him. When Pete stopped sliding he found himself in a gigantic cavern in the middle of nowhere! The cold cavern was too dark and too deep to get out. Pete had no food and no water whatsoever.

In about an hour, he began to get scared and miss his family and best friends. When Pete's friends could not see him, they went back to their penguin village to tell Pete's parents that they could not find him anywhere. As Pete worried and pondered, his family and friends were contemplating a plan to save him. Pete started wandering around to take a good look at the mystical place he was in. He saw crystals and diamonds and rubies! Pete couldn't believe his eyes.

Meanwhile, back in the village, Pete's family and friends slowly retraced Pete's trail. They noticed some sparkly objects flying out of a hole in the slippery snow. It was Pete throwing the jewels. After he threw the diamonds, rubies, and crystals, they magically transformed into a glistening staircase. Pete was able to climb the stairs out to his family and friends!

With the magical jewels, the penguins were able to create an incredible sliding park for everyone to use. Now, the penguins had a safe place to play where no one would get hurt or lost ever again. Pete learned to be more careful in slippery areas and to always know that someone is there to help you.

3rd Place Guest Young Author

Kathleen Kelly
Clearview Regional Middle School
Mantua, New Jersey

The Answer to Autumn

Summer comes to a close in September, but have you ever thought about how the leaves change color? How they fall from the wooden branches? Well, the answer may surprise you.

Chilly winds whispered through the leaves as autumn fast approached. They tried harder than ever, but the autumn leaves just wouldn't fall. By the time sparkly snowflakes fell, the leaves rested on the frosty grass. You are probably wondering how the leaves got there. The answer is… goblins.

Goblins are funny little reptile-like creatures that live in the trunks of trees. They're very grouchy, and their brains are the size of the nuts they drop on little boys' heads. So, let me tell you a nice story.

One autumn night, a village of goblins gathered in the center of the tree trunk. King Goblin stood and got the other goblins' attention.

"Goblins, autumn is here! We must paint the leaves warm colors to make us warmer!" he shouted.

Goblins scrambled in many directions, carrying cans of paint and brushes. They do this because they believe that if they paint the leaves warm colors, they will represent the sun and keep them warm during the chilly winter. All the goblins helped. By morning, every leaf was painted, and everyone slept.

After a few days, the goblins felt no change. In fact, the Goblin Village seemed colder than ever! Goblin King became very angry. He was so angry, he made the entire Goblin Village move to a new tree. He closed the front door with a THUMP!

That night, they painted the leaves, but it did nothing. And every day, they moved into a new tree. After painting every leaf, the king moved the goblins back to their original tree. He tried to think of another way to become warmer, but nothing came into his tiny brain. So, until spring came, the Goblin Village was chilled to the bone. They shook in the icy weather, and so did the trees, and every single leaf fell. So remember to watch out for their "nutty" tricks!

T-Bone's Top Twenty Jersey Shore Websites

1. Nicky Fifth's New Jersey
   www.nickyfifth.com

2. Celebrate New Jersey
   www.celebratenj.org

3. New Jersey Division of Travel and Tourism
   www.visitnj.org

4. Fun New Jersey
   www.funnewjersey.com

5. Historic Cold Spring Village
   www.hcsv.org

6. Cape May
   www.capemay.com

7. Wildwoods
   www.wildwoodsnj.com

8. Sea Isle City
   www.seaislecitynj.us

9. Atlantic City
   www.atlanticcitynj.com

10. Long Beach Island
    www.longbeachisland.com

11. Seaside Heights
    www.seasideheightstourism.com

12. Point Pleasant Beach
www.jenkinsons.com

13. Asbury Park
www.apboardwalk.com

14. Long Branch
www.piervillage.com

15. Sandy Hook
www.sandy-hook.com

16. Keansburg Amusement Park
www.keansburgamusementpark.com

17. Lighthouses - NJ Lighthouse Society
www.njlhs.org

18. New Jersey fun and information
www.nj.gov

19. New Jersey Shore
www.newjerseyshore.com

20. New Jersey Shore
www.nj.com/shore

Nicky Fifth's Favorite New Jersey Books

1. **Our New Jersey** *by Steve Greer*
This hardcover book is filled with amazing pictures and descriptions. Every New Jersey house and classroom should have a copy.

2. **52 Weekends in New Jersey** *by Mitch Kaplan* Great ideas for exploring New Jersey. Call before you visit as this book was published in 2005.

3. **New Jersey Day Trips** *by Patrick Sarver*
Another great guide for exploring the Garden State. Definitely call ahead and make sure listings are still open and that the hours haven't changed.

4. **Barnegat Lighthouse Perspectives** *by David Biggy*
If you think lighthouses are cool, this books has some great pictures of Old Barney.

5. **Crazy Stuff New Jersey** *by Matt Dexter*
Little-known facts about the Garden State and lots of fun learning about them.

6. **New Jersey** *by Laura Kiniry*
This handbook is a great resource for finding cool places and planning your day trips. It covers the entire state.

7. The **Images of America** books
These books are a great snapshot of the history and changes of towns across America. Visit your local book-stores and they will surely have a book about your town

or towns nearby. The pictures are amazing and you can see where towns come from to find a clue about where they are heading. They also have great books about the New Jersey Turnpike, Pine Barrens, and of course, the Jersey Shore.

8. The First Resort: Fun, Sun, Fire, and War in Cape May, America's Original Seaside Town
by Ben Miller

Learn the amazing history of Cape May with pictures and stories. More than Cape May's history, an important part of New Jersey and America's history, too.

9. Cottages and Mansions of the Jersey Shore
by Caroline Seebohm and Peter C. Cook

Great pictures of the Jersey Shore as well as the many different types of homes, from cottages to manisons, that you'll see when you explore.

10. Atlantic City: Now and Then
by Edward Arthur Mauger

See how Atlantic City has changed and grown over the decades and enjoy pictures of now and pictures of then while reading some amazing, real history.

Using the Nicky Fifth Passport

The Nicky Fifth Passport is a great way to follow the adventures of Nicky and T-Bone as they explore New Jersey. Simply arrive at one of the Stamp Stops and present your book. You will receive an N5 stamp in that block of your passport. Since all real New Jersey destinations are used, there are times when a Stamp Stop closes or is unable to stamp your book. In that case, please ask the next Stamp Stop you visit to stamp that block for you.

Visit **www.nickyfifth.com** for Stamp Stop addresses, phone numbers, and information to make finding Stamp Stops and stamping your passport easier.

Tips for Traveling

Plan ahead: Use a map, use the web, call ahead and expect the unexpected, for that's what makes travel fun and exciting.

Take a detour: Your GPS may repeatedly yell "re-calculating," but that's all right. Get off of the highways and see what the *actual towns* look like instead of the *actual signs*.

Plan under: Rather than overplan, underplan. When you underplan, you leave time in your schedule for spontaneous exploration, tired kids, and pit stops. Avoid frustration and plan less than you think you will have time for, *but have a list of possibilities ready for any extra time.*

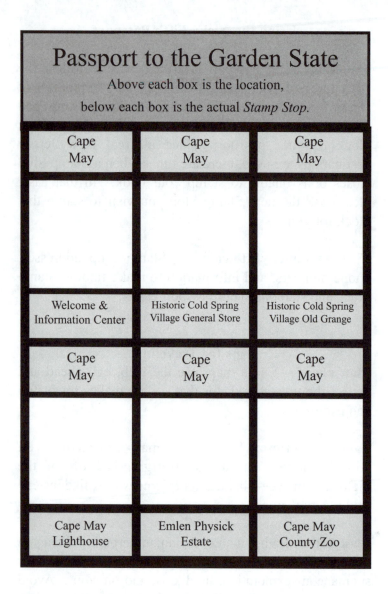

Passport to the Garden State

Above each box is the location,
below each box is the actual *Stamp Stop*.

Cape May	Cape May	Cape May
Welcome & Information Center	Historic Cold Spring Village General Store	Historic Cold Spring Village Old Grange
Cape May	Cape May	Cape May
Cape May Lighthouse	Emlen Physick Estate	Cape May County Zoo

Passport to the Garden State

Above each box is the location,

below each box is the actual *Stamp Stop*.

Wildwood	Wildwood	Stone Harbor
Welcome Center	Hereford Inlet Lighthouse	Pirate Island Mini-Golf
Avalon	Avalon	Sea Isle City
Nemo's Family Restaurant	Pirate Island Mini-Golf	Pirate Island Mini-Golf

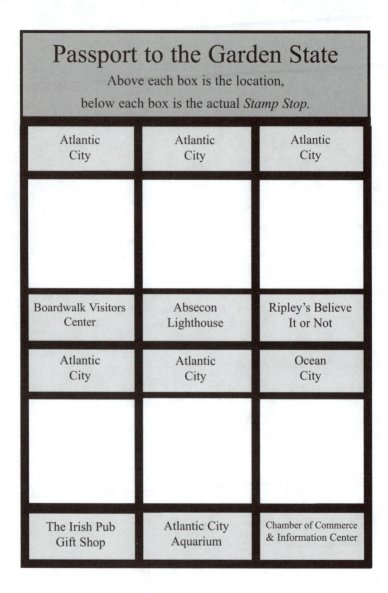

Passport to the Garden State

Above each box is the location,

below each box is the actual *Stamp Stop*.

Atlantic City	Atlantic City	Atlantic City
Boardwalk Visitors Center	Absecon Lighthouse	Ripley's Believe It or Not
Atlantic City	Atlantic City	Ocean City
The Irish Pub Gift Shop	Atlantic City Aquarium	Chamber of Commerce & Information Center

Passport to the Garden State

Above each box is the location,
below each box is the actual *Stamp Stop*.

Ocean City	Ocean City	Long Beach Island
Chatterbox Restaurant	Voltaco's Italian Food	Bill Burr's Flamingo Golf
Long Beach Island	Seaside Heights	Seaside Heights
Scojo's Restaurant	Magical Carousel Shoppe	Sawmill Cafe

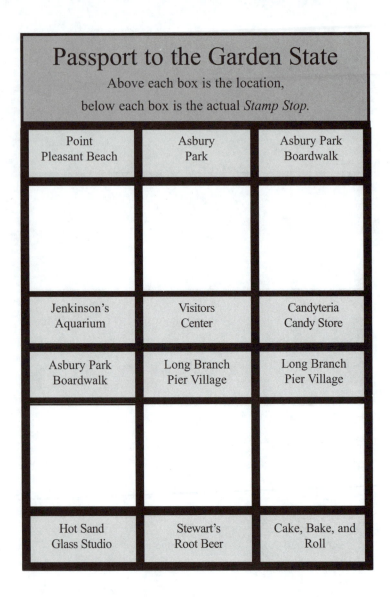

Passport to the Garden State

Above each box is the location,
below each box is the actual *Stamp Stop*.

Point Pleasant Beach	Asbury Park	Asbury Park Boardwalk
Jenkinson's Aquarium	Visitors Center	Candyteria Candy Store
Asbury Park Boardwalk	Long Branch Pier Village	Long Branch Pier Village
Hot Sand Glass Studio	Stewart's Root Beer	Cake, Bake, and Roll

Passport to the Garden State

Above each box is the location,

below each box is the actual *Stamp Stop*.

Sandy Hook	Keansburg	Keansburg
Sea Gulls' Nest Restaurant	Keansburg Amusement Park	Runaway Rapids Water Park
Hamilton Twp. Mercer County	Bordentown	Lawrenceville
Pete's Steakhouse	I Scream, U Scream	Captain Paul's Firehouse Dogs

About the Duke Pediatric Blood & Marrow Transplant Family Support Program

The mission of the Family Support Program (FSP) is to care for, serve, and lighten the burden of the Duke Pediatric Blood and Marrow Transplant (PBMT) community through a comprehensive array of services and resources. The intensity of the transplant process, relocation to Durham for six to eight months, financial and social pressures, and uncertainty about outcome create tremendous anxiety for the families of children undergoing bone marrow and stem cell transplants. In 1997, to help families cope, the Family Support Program was established within the Duke PBMT program.

The Family Support Program seeks to meet the physical, emotional, social, and financial needs of PBMT patients and their families through 25 ongoing programs. Support is offered to PBMT families on a consistent basis throughout their stay in Durham through the FSP and the staff maintains relationships with families when they leave Durham. Because of families' precarious financial situations and in order that they might be able to focus on the care and well-being of their child, FSP provides funds for everyday needs such as food, taxis, gas cards, prescription co-payments, and utility bills. Every year, families are invited to join the PBMT community for a weekend celebration and remembrance of the lives of transplanted children at the Rainbow of Heroes Walk.

Visit **www.rainbowofheroeswalk.org** to help.

About the Author

Lisa Funari Willever wanted to be an author since she was in the third grade and often says if there was a Guest Young Author contest when she was a child, she would have submitted a story a day. Maybe even two a day on weekends!

She has been a wedding dress seller, a file clerk, a sock counter (really), a hostess, waitress, teacher, and author. While she loved teaching in Trenton, New Jersey, becoming an author has been one of the most exciting adventures of her life. She is a full-time mom and a night-time author who travels all over the world visiting schools. She has been to hundreds of schools in dozens of states, including California, South Dakota, Iowa, South Carolina, North Carolina, Florida, Delaware, Connecticut, New York, Pennsylvania, West Virginia, Ohio, Nevada, Idaho, Utah, Alabama, Louisiana, and even the U.S. Navy base in Sasebo, Japan.

Lisa has written seventeen books for children and new teachers. *A Glove of Their Own* won the 2009 Benjamin Franklin Award and *There's a Kid Under My Bed* was a 2009 Foreword Magazine's Book of the Year finalist. Critically-acclaimed *Chumpkin* was selected as a favorite by First Lady Laura Bush and displayed at the White House, *Everybody Moos at Cows* was featured on the Rosie O'Donnell Show, and *Garden State Adventure* and *32 Dandelion Court* have been selections for the prestigious New Jersey Battle of the Books list. Her other titles include: *Nicky Fifth For Hire, Passport to the Garden State, You Can't Walk a Fish, The Easter Chicken, Maximilian the Great, Where Do Snowmen Go?, The Culprit Was a Fly, Miracle on Theodore's Street, Exciting Writing,* and *On Your Mark, Get Set, Teach*.

Lisa, a graduate of Trenton State College and is married to Todd Willever, a captain in the Trenton Fire Department. They reside in Mansfield, New Jersey with their three children, Jessica, Patrick, and Timothy.

If you would like to invite Lisa to your school, visit www.franklinmasonpress.com for more details.